STORIES FROM LAST WEDNESDAY

Claremore, OK

Copyright © 2018 Spacebar Publishing, LLC
All rights reserved.
Second edition, August 2018
ISBN-13: 978-1-7323007-4-3

No part of this publication may be reproduced or distributed in print or electronic form without prior permission of the author.

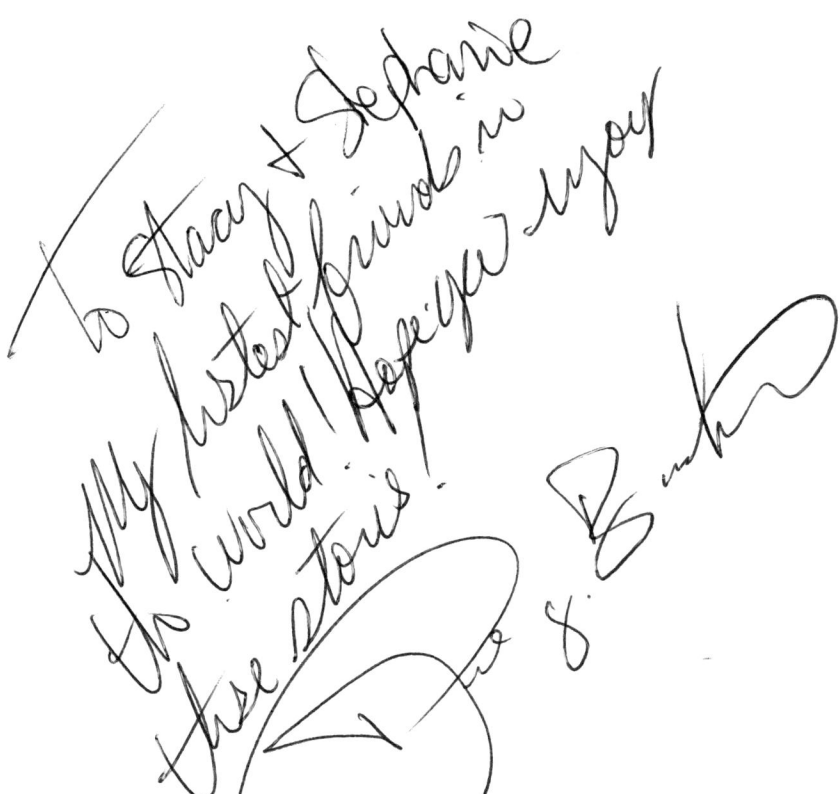

For the art of storytelling and the power of a group coming together to accomplish a goal

Foreword

A little more than a year ago, I had the honor of teaching a short story class at Northeast Technology Center in Claremore, Oklahoma. After the first two classes, I realized I was no longer the teacher, only a facilitator. In fact, all the students who enrolled in the class are better writers than I am.

During the six-week class, it came out everyone had a novel in their heads. We decided to start a writing group to help each other out. Thus, Last Wednesday Writers was born.

A few months ago, we decided to publish an anthology of short stories. Some of the stories started in our class, while others were born since then. Each short story features the diverse talent of each member of our group. From fantasy and science fiction, to adventure and everyday life, I am sure you will find a short story you will love.

Thank you for taking the time to read our stories. If you like them, tell your friends. If you don't like them, don't tell anyone!

~Mark Cook

These stories are works of fiction. All names, characters, institutions, places, and events portrayed in each story are either products of the author's imagination or are used fictitiously. Any resemblance to actual persons, living or dead, business establishments, or events is entirely coincidental.

CONTENTS

1. FRITTER 1
2. HOW WOLF LEARNED TO HOWL 17
3. THE GAMES 21
4. LATE… AGAIN 37
5. LORD WILLING AND THE CREEK DON'T RISE 50
6. MY NAME IS EMMA 66
7. NIGHT CREATURE 74
8. THE LOST GOLD MINE OF IDAHO SPRINGS 82
9. HALLOW FOREST 160
10. SCRUBBED 201

ABOUT THE AUTHORS 229

ACKNOWLEDGMENTS
Cover Photo by Paul G Buckner
Special thanks to Debbie and Alger at Northeast Technology Center

1. FRITTER
By MARK COOK

Perhaps there is nothing harder than losing a good friend. In the summer of my twelfth year, I met and lost the best friend a boy could ever have.

The morning had been rough. Rounding up the cows for morning feeding took twice as long, and to top it off, I lost my favorite hat.

By the time I got the cows herded to the barn, the sun was sneaking over Eldon Mountain. Once the cows were in the holding lot, I went inside the barn and gathered the green, plastic five-gallon buckets I used to haul the feed from the bin to the trough. The smell of fresh manure, wet cows, and fly killer aerosol hung in the air.

I flipped the latch up on the back door, walked around the wooden deck to the feed bin, and froze. There, under the gnarled arms of the pin oak tree that provided shade for the barn, and was the favorite route of squirrels to the feed bin, lay the meanest looking dog I ever saw. Its belly pooched out like a pregnant heifer.

The crimson fur ball looked like he was part chow, but

he was no pureblood. Only his tail, neck, and tongue were chow, the rest of him was pure mutt. His sleek coat glistened in the sunlight as he finished off what looked to be an armadillo. What Texans call possum on the half shell. When he saw me he stood up, his tail hung between his legs, his teeth escaping from under his lips. The noise out of his throat made the hair on my neck stand straight up and sent a wave of goosebumps scrambling all the way down to my toes.

"Whoa, there boy," I said, easing backward to the door. "I won't hurt you." He didn't seem too concerned about me hurting him. The devil dog stopped growling, but still showed his teeth. They looked plenty sharp.

"You go ahead and finish eating. I'll come back later." I jumped back into the barn and slammed the door shut.

"James, where's the feed?" Gramps shouted from the milking room. "Hurry up, before these heifers start bawlin' their heads off."

"Sorry, Gramps, but there's a big red dog out back and he don't seem none too friendly!" I hollered back.

"He won't bother you none as long as you don't bother him."

I opened the door just wide enough to peek out. The dog was gone. Only the shell remained of the armadillo. I opened the door wider and eased out onto the wooden deck. I grabbed the two buckets and filled them to the top with sweet smelling corn feed, stopping several times to make sure the dog wasn't sneaking up on me.

"Whose dog is he?" I asked Gramps as I hauled the feed to the trough and dumped it. The cows mooing their gratitude almost drowned out Gramps answer.

"He's nobody's dog. He just showed up here one day about a month ago. I reckon somebody dumped him." Gramps was bent over hooking up the milkers to a Jersey's udders. "You leave that dog be. He don't want anything to do with humans."

Gramps moved onto the next cow and began washing the dirt off her udders with a wet rag. "I've been trying to make friends with him since he showed up and he won't let me get within ten yards of him. I even tried to coax him with a weenie. He wouldn't have any of it. He musta been treated bad by somebody." Gramps hooked the milkers to the cow and then rose up and patted the cow on the rear. "That dog just don't like people." He seemed to notice my bare head for the first time.

"Where's your hat?"

"Ahh, that big old sycamore down by the creek snagged it when I jumped across this mornin'," I said, setting the buckets down by the back door. "I didn't wanna take time trying to find it in the dark, so I left it. I'll go get it after lunch." Gramps laughed and told me to bring in the next batch of cows from the holding lot.

Altogether we milked nearly a hundred cows twice a day, once early in the morning and again late in the evening. When we weren't milking cows, there were fences to mend, hay to cut, bale and haul, and a thousand others things to ensure we wouldn't get bored. This was my grandparents' dairy farm.

Every summer, since I was a kid, I went to live with them. It's what I looked forward to all year long. The work was hard, but I also got to fish, hunt, and explore the Cherokee Hills that grew up around Eldon Valley.

After lunch, I excused myself from the table, grabbed my .22 and headed down the hill towards the creek. The sun was at its peak, and the thick June air caused my t-shirt to grip my back like a clammy fist. I made it to the shade of the oak tree and the coolness of the creek as fast as I could.

Somewhere along the bank, I would find my cap. I wasn't

a big Chiefs fan, but Gramps was, and he gave it to me last year for my eleventh birthday. I sat down under a large oak tree to rest, looking first to make sure there was no poison ivy.

This was one of my favorite places to come and just relax. Soft grass made the perfect sleeping pad, while moss-covered roots from the oak tree provided the perfect pillow. The serene noise of the creek flowing over sleek, white sand stones was the ultimate lullaby. Songbirds sang their familiar songs, while feisty squirrels played in the canopy above me. I laid my head down on the blanket of moss and closed my eyes.

Just as I nodded off, I heard something rustling in the brush down the creek aways. It was the devil dog. He had a rabbit in his mouth and was crossing the creek when he saw me. He froze, and then after a few seconds, continued across about thirty yards from me.

"Hey boy, how you doin' boy?" I said, trying to hide my fear. "Whatcha got there, lunch?" The dog dropped the rabbit and ambled forward a few steps until he was standing right over it. He didn't growl, but he definitely wasn't going to invite me to join him. "Hey I was just leavin'. You enjoy your lunch and I'll be seein' you."

I backed away from him, turned and walked slowly back to the house, tensing my back muscles, expecting an attack. When I was almost back to the house I got up enough courage to look back. He was gone. I sighed with relief and walked through the front yard. Gramps sat in his favorite rocker on the front porch.

"Where's your hat? I thought you was going lookin' for it?"

"I was, then I figured I better get that pole on the holdin' corral fixed, so the cows won't get out," I said, embarrassed that I was afraid of a stupid old dog.

"Well, that's a fine idea. You can look for that ole hat anytime." I could tell Gramps knew something was wrong and was letting me off easy.

I went in the house and headed towards my room. The smell from Grandma's kitchen changed my mind. Those fancy pastry chefs in Europe couldn't hold a candle to the heavenly smell coming from the big pot on the stove. Grandma stood over the pot, her bowl of batter next to her, dipping apple slices into the batter and then into the hot oil. The finished product was the best tasting apple fritters in the county.

"Why James, I didn't know you was here," she said, wiping her forehead with the tail of her apron. "Gramps said you was off lookin' for your hat."

"I was, but then I decided I better fix the holdin' corral."

"Well, take some fritters with you to give you energy."

"Thanks, Grandma, I will."

I grabbed a paper bag from under the counter and loaded it with fritters covered in powdered sugar, while Grandma stood with her mouth hanging open. I don't think she planned on me taking the whole batch. I ran out of the house and down to the milk barn. I walked through the front door, out to the feed bin and then to the holding pen. I didn't think it would take long to fix the corral, so I set the paper bag full of fritters on the corral post and walked across the barnyard to the woodshed.

When I came back, that darn dog was laying on the ground, his whole head stuffed in the paper sack. I was so mad, I forgot I was afraid of him. "Git! You sorry excuse for a dog!"

Startled, the thieving dog jerked his head out of the bag, and faced me. His whole muzzle was covered with powdered sugar and a grin spread across it. I ran at him

FRITTER

yelling and cursing and chunking anything I could get my hands on at him. He just laid there scratching his ear with his hind foot. Halfway across the barnyard I tripped over a rock and went down on my face. I swear I heard that fritter-stealing dog laugh. I grabbed a fist-sized rock and threw it at him. I missed, but it was close enough to let him know I wasn't playing. He slowly got to his feet, stretched his legs, and trotted away.

"Darn dog!" I hollered after him.

When I made it over to the bag, I knew that dad burn dog had eaten my whole bag of fritters. I picked up the torn sack and threw it in the trash barrel. "I'll get you back you stupid dog!" I muttered under my breath, and then gathered up my tools and finished fixing the holding pen fence.

When I went back to the house, Gramps was sitting on the front porch eating apple fritters and drinking milk. Grandma sat next to him hulling beans. I told them about that stinking dog eating my fritters. Gramps laughed so hard milk went up his nose and all down the bib of his overalls. "That stupid, thievin', no account, fritter-stealin' dog is going to get his though," I said promised. "You just wait and see. Next time I get him in the sites of my .22, I'm going to send him to the Promised Land."

"You leave that dog alone," Gramps said when he finally quit laughing. "You shouldn't have taken that whole batch of fritters anyway. And 'sides, Fritter was just doing what comes natural."

"Fritter! Now you've gone and named him Fritter?" I couldn't believe it. That darn dog stole from me, and now Gramps is making light of me by naming him, Fritter!

"All that darn dog does is a steal. I'm goin' to put an end to his stealin' ways. Those will be the last apple fritters that dog ever swipes from me."

"You'll do no such thing!" Grandma said as she broke open a shell and dropped the brown beans into her bowl. "Fritter may be a thief, but since he's been around, those wild dogs haven't killed uh one of my chickens. He's earned his keep." Grandma gave me the look all grandmothers seem to pass on down to their daughters: that you-better-listen-to-me-or-I'm-going-to-set-the-rear-end-of-your-pants-afire look.

"All right Grandma, I won't shoot him, but dadgummit why do we have to keep him around?" I asked, backing down from Grandma's stern stare. "He'll steal everything I've got."

For the next month, I tried to make friends with Fritter. I figured it would be better to have him as a friend than an enemy, especially since Grandma wouldn't let me shoot him. The only problem was Fritter didn't want me getting close. The closest I got to Fritter was when I had an apple fritter in my hand. I coaxed and sweet-talked him 'til he was within a few feet. But even an apple fritter has limited power. Fritter wouldn't get any closer. I started to walk toward him, and he backed up.

"Fine, if you don't want it, you don't have to have it." I acted like I was eating it, but he was no fool. After weeks of trying to be Fritter's friend, I finally gave up. I wanted him to hunt and play in the creek with me, like most dogs would, but if he wouldn't, he wouldn't.

At the same time I was trying to be Fritter's friend, I also kept looking for my cap. It was nowhere to be found. I looked all around the creek; it was gone. I didn't want Gramps to be mad at me so I kept looking for it. One time I started to go look for it, and Gramps caught me going out the back door. "Where you goin'?"

Tired of trying to keep the secret, I told him about the hat. He didn't have much to say other than to be careful.

FRITTER

The pack of wild dogs that had been stealing all over the valley was getting braver. They had killed two of Mr. Rawlings' finest coon dogs just the other night.

"Take your gun with you just in case you see 'um."

"All right." I usually took my .22 anyway.

"Be back before evening milking. I may need you to start the milking."

"How come?"

"We got a calf missing. I'm afraid them dogs mighta killed it. I'm gonna go see if I can find it."

I left Gramps reading the paper and hiked to the creek. After a couple of hours searching for my cap, I sat down by the old oak tree and watched two squirrels fight over an acorn like two kids fighting over a Hershey bar. Suddenly, Fritter came plunging through the brush, dragging his hind legs behind him, my Kansas City Chiefs cap in his mouth. I eased around the big oak tree and put the strong, gray trunk between us. I don't think he saw me. He laid on the bank near the water, his breathing ragged. I crawled toward the bank above where Fritter lounged.

As I peered over the edge, I heard Fritter whimper. I could see why. His whole right side was covered in blood. His hind leg nearly torn off at the hip. I slid down the gravel bank and crept up on him. He raised his head and showed me his teeth; a soft growl came from deep within.

"It's okay boy. I won't hurt you," I whispered as I edged closer.

What I saw when I got closer almost made me sick. Fritter's throat was torn open, and his right leg was barely attached. His face had a long cut on it that ran from just below his eye to the tip of his nose. Thick red blood oozed from his throat and leg. I took off my shirt and dipped it in the water. I held the shirt above Fritter's mouth and gently squeezed. He lapped up the water like a calf who missed breakfast. His breathing was slow, and he seemed to be calming down.

"It's okay boy. You'll be alright," I lied. I knew there was nothing I could do for Fritter and I think he knew it too. I couldn't help him, and he would never survive the trip to Gramp's house.

Fritter whimpered and looked at me with sad eyes. I ran my hand along his smooth fur and scratched gently behind his ears. He nuzzled my other hand, raised his head to look me in the eyes and then lowered it. The last of his air escaped his lungs like air from a balloon.

"What happened to you boy? What did this to you?" I said, wiping my eyes dry on my sleeve.

I put my cap on, grabbed my .22 and ran to the house. Grandma was in the kitchen canning preserves; the pressure cooker hissed on the stove. Mason jars covered the table, and blocks of paraffin sat on the counter. The smell of strawberry preserves was so sweet it was almost sickening. Grandma looked at me and nearly fainted. Fritter's blood covered my overalls. "It's okay Grandma. It's not my blood, it's Fritter's."

I spent the next few minutes telling her about finding Fritter. "I'm sorry about Fritter. I know you liked him," she said as she grabbed my hand and held it. "I see you found your hat."

"No, Fritter found it. Where's Gramps?" I said, collapsing in the kitchen chair.

"He's still out looking for the calf. It seems like those wild dogs will never die. No matter how many times Gramps and the other farmers hunt them down and kill them, there's always more to take their place." Grandma reached into the fridge, pulled out a jug of milk and poured me a tall glass. "Seems like they're gettin' braver too. They got Mr. Rawlings' coon dogs, and Millie Brinks told me they attacked her dogs right in their pen. Would uh killed 'em too if Paul hadn't come out of the house with his shotgun and killed one of 'em."

"How long has Gramps been gone?" I asked after downing the glass of milk.

"Since right after you left. Come to think of it, Gramps shoulduh been back before now. I'm surprised you two didn't cross paths."

"I'll go look for him." I stood and gathered my cap and rifle.

"You be back before supper. And tell Gramps he still hasn't fixed my clothesline," she shouted as I went out the back door and headed down the hill.

I searched for what seemed like hours before I discovered any sign of Gramps. In the soft mud near a cow path, I found his footprints. Gramps always wore work boots with deep tread. There was no doubt these were his.

I followed the tracks to the far end of the hay meadow. About a hundred yards away, under the deep shade of a stand of oak trees, the cows were bunched facing the pond. The only time cows bunched like that were at night or for protection. I was starting to get scared, not for myself, but for Gramps. As fast as I could, I ran toward the cows. They heard me just before I got there. Some turned their heads toward me, but seeing no danger, they quickly turned back toward the pond.

"Gramps, you around here?" I hollered above the snorts and moos of the cows. "Gramps! You better answer if you can hear me." The only answer was a calf crying. "Grandma is mighty mad at you for not fixin' her clothesline. Gramps!"

There was still no answer, so I started into the woods and had only gone about fifty feet when I heard the growls. At first, they were low and then grew louder and seemed to echo. Only it wasn't an echo. It was coming from another place. I chambered a round in my .22 and aimed toward the brush. "Get outta there! Hiyaa! Get!" The growls grew louder and seemed to multiply.

From the far side of the cows, I heard the bull snort and then charge. I heard a yelp and then saw a black and white ball of fur hit the bank of the pond and roll three times. When the wild dog stopped, it didn't move. Brush popping brought me back to my predicament. From the growling, it seemed the dogs had me surrounded. An ugly brown dog ran at me from the woods to my left.

"Hiyaa!" I hollered as loud as I could. The dog stopped and looked at me in confusion. I confused him even more when I raised the rifle and shot him through the chest. From my right a big, powerful dog that looked like a German Shepherd came at me. I cocked my lever action Henry and fired. My shot hit him, but didn't slow him down. I ejected the shell and chambered another round. My second shot flew true and struck the dog in the mouth, dropping him in his tracks.

The other dogs seemed to learn from their dead friends' mistakes. I could hear them pacing and growling, but no target presented itself. I headed toward the pond. If nothing else, I could put the pond to my back and only have to face the wild dogs from three directions. Plus my mouth was as dry as a desert rattlesnake's belly.

When I got to the pond, I bent down on one knee, cupped my hands and scooped up a handful of water. The water tasted like dead skunk, but at least it was wet. While I finished the last of the water, I heard a moaning sound. I couldn't see what was making the noise, but it didn't sound like an animal. I levered another round in the chamber and crept toward the noise.

It was Gramps. He had dug a shallow hole in the pond

bank and crawled inside. I ran to Gramps, laid my rifle next to him and shook his arm. "Gramps! Are you okay?" There was no answer. "Gramps wake up. Wake up!" Gramps' head had a cut on it and sweat was soaking through his hat.

I reached for his cap to get him some water when I noticed Gramps' left leg. It was twisted the wrong way and blood covered his pant leg. I took out my Old Timer pocket knife and cut the pants leg. I nearly gagged when I saw his leg. The bone had broken through the skin just below the knee and blood oozed out of the dirty opening. Gramps moaned again.

"Wake up Gramps, wake up! You really done it to yourself good this time. I gotta get you some water and then get you outta here." I slid down the bank and filled the cap. I was just turning around when I saw a black streak running at me. It was a huge dog, with folded ears and brown splotches scattered all over him. I reached for my rifle, but it wasn't there. I left it back with Gramps.

"Hiya!" I screamed, hoping to scare it like I did that other dog. But he kept coming and was within 20 feet of me when I heard a shot. The dog flew sideways and laid still. I looked up the bank and saw Gramps sitting up, my rifle gripped loosely from his big hands.

"Gramps!" I hollered and ran to him.

"Don't forget that water, boy," he bellowed before I had gone five steps. I did a three-sixty and grabbed the water-filled cap with both hands. Carrying the water like fragile eggs, I made it to Gramps and handed him the hat.

"Thanks, boy," Gramps said as he gulped down the water. He tried to sit up better and grimaced in pain when his bad leg moved. "My throat is drier than a backseat Baptist's wallet at collection time." He drank the last of the water and asked how I found him.

"Just luck. Them wild dogs almost had me surrounded. I killed a few and was able to make it to the pond. Then I heard you moaning."

"You best keep that rifle close by. Those dogs are after blood. I've never seen dogs act like this, even wild ones." Pain took over Gramps. It was a few minutes before he could talk and then it was through gritted teeth. "Usually they'd be too afraid to try to bring down a man."

"How'd you break your leg?"

"Them dogs done it. I came out here to find that Jersey calf. I found it over yonder on the other side of Bare Rock Hill. The dogs got it. I was just starting to head back when one of them crazy dogs came out of nowhere and knocked me down the hill. I musta broke my leg on that big rock. It probably would have had me if Fritter hadn't shown up."

"Fritter?"

"Yeah, that crazy Fritter came outta nowhere and lit into it. He had the dog by the throat and was popping him like a whip." Gramps' breathing was ragged; he needed a doctor bad. "After he finished that one he took off after the rest of the pack. Don't know if he found them or not. I crawled to the pond and dug me a hole for protection; then I guess I passed out."

"Fritter is dead, Gramps. I found him this morning. He was pretty torn up, but he let me try to doctor him and give him water."

"That's too bad. Fritter was a good dog, mighty skittish around people, but he was a good dog. He saved my hide, that's for sure," Gramps sighed.

"I need more water."

I ran down to the pond and filled my hat. When I came back, I told him about finding Fritter and what kind of shape he was in. "When I found him he had my cap," I said, holding back tears.

"Well, I'll be dad gummed."

"What?"

"I reckon that dog knew he was dyin' and wanted to be close to you. I figure he really liked you. There was something in his past that wouldn't let him trust people. I 'magin you was the first person he liked."

Gramps took another drink of water, and then careful not to move his leg, laid down on his back. "I watched you with that dog. Every time he saw you his whole body wagged." Gramps stopped talking and rested for a moment. "You could see in his eyes that he wanted to run up to you and give you a good lickin'. He musta run across your cap on his way home. I reckon he kept it cause he wanted to die with your smell near him. That's probably as close to affection as he could get."

The whole time Gramps talked I could hear the dogs circling closer and closer.

I was close to breaking down and bawling like a baby. Instead, I grabbed my rifle, chambered a round and ran into the woods, screaming curses at the dogs as loud as I could. With tear-flooded eyes, I shot as fast as I could aim and pull the trigger. I knocked down two dogs and would have hit another if my rifle hadn't jammed. I took out my pocket knife, dug the swollen spent shell out of the chamber, inserted another round and began searching for a new target. The dogs were gone.

I left Gramps and ran back to the barn to get a wagon.. It took awhile, but I finally got Gramps loaded and we headed for home. Grandma saw us coming and ran out of the house to help me with Gramps. "You old fool, what did you do to yourself this time?" She sounded mad, but I could tell she was worried.

"Well old woman," Gramps said, trying to act just as

mad. "I been teachin' young James here how to fight wild dogs. You got supper ready or did you already throw it out?"

"I shoulda thrown it out, but I been keepin' it in the oven. First thing we gotta do is get you to town and to the doctor. That leg looks bad."

We took Gramps to town and got back home late that night. The doctor wanted to put Gramps in the hospital, but he wouldn't have it. He said there was too much work to do.

The next morning, I got up early and rounded up the cows for milking. I took my rifle with me in case the dogs wanted to fight some more, but they didn't. I had to do my chores and Gramps' since he was laid up. It took me until noon to milk the cows, clean the barn and load the feed in the troughs for the evening milking. Gramps was sitting in his rocker on the porch when I got back to the house.

"Lunch is ready. Go on in and get yourself something to eat. You gotta be near starved by now."

"I'm alright. I want to go bury Fritter before the dogs or coyotes get to him," I said, knocking the dust off my overalls with my cap.

"That's a fine idea. I wish I could go with you. That dog saved my bacon and I won't never forget it."

"I gotta go," I said and then turned to walk away.

"Take your rifle. Them dogs might come back."

I went to my room to fetch my rifle. I also took the blanket off my bed; the one Grandma made for me when I was just a baby. When I walked by the kitchen, Grandma was making apple fritters. I walked in and without saying a word filled a sack with apple fritters and walked out of the house, carrying the blanket, my rifle, and the fritters. Next, I went to the toolshed and got a shovel.

I was glad to see Fritter undisturbed. No varmints had

FRITTER

tried to make a meal out of him. Maybe they had respect for a true warrior.

I laid my rifle and the shovel down, sat next to Fritter, and stroked his soft fur. "Fritter, I wanna thank you for savin' Gramps. He's an ornery ol' cuss, but he's the only Gramps I got." I dipped a corner of the blanket in the creek and cleaned the blood off Fritter as much as I could. "I just want you to know you were a great dog. The finest dog in this county, and maybe in the country."

Tears swelled up in my eyes, and it was getting hard to talk without my voice breaking. "I don't know why you were afraid to trust people, but I reckon you had your reasons. I brung you your favorite, apple fritters. Grandma made 'em fresh today. I reckon they'll keep you from getting' too hungry on your trip to heaven. You take care of them angels up there."

Blinded by tears, I dug Fritter's grave. When I finished, I patted his head, wrapped him in my blanket, and laid him down gently in the hole. Then I took off my hat and laid it in the hole next to Fritter.

"This is a fine spot." I filled the hole with rich, black dirt and walked home.

2. HOW WOLF LEARNED TO HOWL
By JULIE JONES

Many summers ago when Wolf was young, he was padding through the forest on a fine day when he heard a beautiful song coming from the treetops. He stopped to listen, and as he gazed at the canopy above he saw a mockingbird perched on a branch.

"Mockingbird!" Wolf called. "Your song is so lovely! Won't you teach me to sing it, too?"

Mockingbird was pleased at Wolf's praise for he knew he could sing beautifully, and he agreed to teach Wolf what he knew.

"Of course!" he said, flying to a lower branch so Wolf could hear. "First, try this."

Mockingbird trilled a pure note into the morning air. Wolf was impressed and tried to imitate Mockingbird's sound.

"Aaaaooooooooooo!" he ventured.

Mockingbird cringed at the harsh sound but fluffed his feathers and tried again with a different note. Again, Wolf tried his best but could not match the loveliness of

HOW WOLF LEARNED TO HOWL

Mockingbird's song.

"No, no no," Mockingbird admonished. "You're putting far too much throat in it. Sing from your belly! Try again!"

Over and over all through the morning, Wolf tried as best he could to match Mockingbird's effortless music but was never able to utter anything other than a high-pitched howl. As the day wore on, Wolf noticed that many other animals had gathered to watch the failing lesson and he began to feel ashamed of his terrible voice.

At length Wolf said to Mockingbird, "It's no use. I will never be able to sing like you."

Mockingbird felt bad for his new friend. "Maybe you just need more practice?" he said, hopeful.

"With a voice like that, practice won't do any good!" Rabbit announced, and all the other animals laughed.

"Yeah, why don't you just give it up now?" Badger said, in his typical sour way.

Wolf was embarrassed and slunk away from the other animals to hide his shame in the forest. He walked and walked, thinking as he went. He began to wonder if Mockingbird was right about needing more practice. He stopped next to a stream, and after a drink to wet his throat he tried again.

"Aaaaoooooooooooo!" he howled.

"Gahhh, can you *not* make such an abominable noise, please?"

The voice came from behind a nearby bush, and Wolf jumped in surprise. A few moments later, Tortoise came ambling into view.

"Hello, Tortoise," Wolf said. "I'm sorry if my singing disturbed you."

Tortoise snorted in derision. "Sonny boy, if that's what you call singing I suggest you find another hobby," he said.

Wolf watched as Tortoise turned and made his lumbering way along the trail.

Wolf was more dejected than ever. He kept walking, stopping every little while to try his song but always there was an animal nearby that heard and complained, or even worse, laughed.

At last Wolf came to a tall hill and climbed up to the very top. When he reached the peak, he looked around and saw that it was full night. He had been walking and trying to sing for the entire day and he still had not made a single noise that sounded like Mockingbird. Wolf was so sad that he raised his muzzle to the sky and let out one long final howl.

"Hello there," a kind voice said, and for the second time Wolf was surprised. He looked all around but could see no other animals.

"I like your singing very much," the voice said.

Wolf was beside himself. He looked and looked for the source of the voice, and at last the voice told him to look up.

There in the sky hung Moon, silent and bright and alone. She flashed Wolf a kind smile and he found himself smiling back.

"Will you sing for me again?" Moon asked.

Wolf felt his smile fade. "I can't sing," he said. "You're just being nice."

"Not at all," Moon said. "I think you have a fine voice. It gets very lonely here in the sky, night after night, with nobody to talk to. Most of the animals are asleep, and the ones that aren't sleeping are quiet and secretive. It's very hard to make friends."

This made Wolf sad for Moon. He resolved to become her companion and keep her company through the long nights. Smiling at his new friend, Wolf raised his nose and

HOW WOLF LEARNED TO HOWL

let out the longest, loudest howl he had ever tried. Moon laughed in delight, and Wolf joined in, for he had learned that no matter how you sing, someone out there will love your music.

3. THE GAMES
By JOHN D KETCHER JR

Since the takeover of the government by the new political party, the Liberal Nationalist Party, all other parties were declared illegal and the leadership of those parties arrested. They were replaced by hand-picked loyalists from the DNC. The bloodless coup was over in 24 hours with the help of the National Guard and local law enforcement. All elected officials, state and federal, were arrested and jailed until their usefulness could be determined.

The National News Syndicates for the past several years had kept up the daily barrage of fake news to turn the people against the Republican Party and those who supported the Republicans. On the day of the coup all news agencies went silent for 24 hours. Fox News and affiliates were shut down permanently and its employees arrested.

Day 2 of the coup all churches were closed and doors locked. Pastors were required to provide a list of all church members to the new local authorities of each city or town. That evening the National News Syndicates returned to its

THE GAMES

regular broadcasting. Each news station played a prerecorded statement from the new government. The speaker was a former president.

"*My fellow Americans, over the last several years the current President and Republican Party has devastated our economy and way of life. Our nation was on the verge collapse, health care cost rising and unaffordable and on the brink of war with China, North Korea and Russia. In good conscience we could not allow that to happen. Therefore, a group of loyal citizens came together to put a stop to the chaos and have formed a new government…"*

***

Six months later

The stadium filled up fast. People kept pouring in. The local high school band provided music for the event. There was a little bit of Rock n Roll, some Swing and Country to satisfy the listening ear of most all generations. Some arrived early and enjoyed tailgating. The aroma from the steaks and burgers being grilled greeted people as they walked through the parking lot to the stadium entrance.

The excitement had been building for this special event- The Games. Vendors made a killing selling popcorn, roasted nuts and drinks to the crowd. Now the climax of the anticipated event was at hand.

A black limousine appeared from the east entrance of the stadium and continued down the sideline to the fifty yard line where it stopped in front of a platform. The band plays "We will Rock You." The crowd cheers. The driver jumped out and opened the back passenger door and a middle-aged lady exited the vehicle outfitted in a brown shirt with matching trousers, a black tie and black combat boots. A tall similar dressed man followed. Both waved as they climb the stairs to the top of the platform. The mayor of the town introduced himself and shook their hands. Once the greetings were over they took their seats and waited for the band to finish.

Mayor Henry H. Monroe moved to the podium and addressed the people. "Ladies and gentlemen. We are here this evening to celebrate the victory over our enemies. These Enemies of the State have eroded our way of life. They have led many astray with their false beliefs and denied all Americans their right to Life, Liberty and Pursuit of Happiness. But all that changed, when true American Patriots stood up and said 'No more!' and they took back control for all the American people. Tonight, two of these true American Patriots are with us. I introduce to you our District Commander Terry McVile and her husband Patrick McVile, District Overseer of the Games."

The crowd goes wild and gave a standing ovation for the honored guests. Once again, the couple wave to the people then the District Commander approaches the podium.

"Thank you all for the warm reception. We've come a long way in our battle against our enemies. But people like you, here tonight, made the fighting much easier. We have been able to disband all political parties and have outlawed all church denominations. We have structured a new party. There is but one party and that is the Liberal Nationalist Party. We worship no other god but the Liberal Nationalist Party." The crowd erupts with shouts of joy while the band struck up another tune.

"Thank you again. The Enemies of the State are running, but we will never stop hunting them down. Tonight, we are going to give some of them an opportunity to renounce their affiliation with these outlaw parties." She paused for effect. "Because we are a benevolent party we

THE GAMES

will also give Christians a chance to renounce their faith in their false god. Those that renounce their affiliation and faith will be sent to re-education camps and later returned home as obedient and productive citizens of the Liberal Nationalist Party. To those who will not renounce, they will be put to death. Here. Tonight." The crowd goes wild.

The District Commander points to the ten-foot-high security fence with razor wire on top surrounding the playing field. Inside stood 500 men, women and children. The prisoners were weeping and wailing. Parents holding up their children, begging for mercy. Others falling prostrate on the ground, no longer having the strength to stand on their own. All had been held in concentration camps scattered throughout Oklahoma for the past five months and during that time they had not showered nor changed clothing. The aroma of their collective filth and body odor drifted over the stadium causing the witnesses to tonight's game to wave their hands in front of their noses in an attempt to ward off the stink.

"These are the first of thousands in Oklahoma, who will play in these monthly events. Now let The Games begin!" Stepping back from the microphone she scanned the pitiful group in front of her.

Her eyes stopped and focused on a small group of people.

In the midst of the chaos was a group of men, women and children kneeling in prayer. Standing in the center was an old man with arms stretched out and face lifted upward to heaven leading the prayer.

"Security! Stop them now." Screamed the District Commander.

All eyes turned to see what the District Commander was screaming about.

JOHN D KETCHER JR

***

Security stormed the fenced in area with raised batons. Running through the crowd their batons connected with heads, arms and torsos. Bodies fell. Screaming erupted. People scrambled to distance themselves from those praying. Finally, only the old man was left standing. The security team stood around him, poised to rush him but stopped dead in their tracks. Something prevented them from advancing. A bright light began emanating around the old man causing them to raise their hands to shield their eyes.

The light shone so bright the people in the stadium also had to shield their eyes. Even the district commander turned her head.

"Why do you harm us? We are no threat to you. We are making peace with the Almighty before we die." Said the old man.

Silence.

His voice reminds me of my grandfather when I did something wrong. It was neither condemning nor accusing but of sadness. The Security Chief thought. Cautiously he lowered his hand from his eyes and motioned for his team to leave the area. Taking one last look at the old man, he turned and followed his men.

The mayor sat motionless afraid to show any emotion to the cruelty displayed on the field. He was just thankful to be on the podium and not one of the 500.

"That's better. There's no praying except to the Liberal Nationalist Party." The District Commander then shifted her focus to the old man. "You look familiar. Who are you?"

"Pastor Eagle."

"Yes. I remember. You had some hateful things to say

THE GAMES

about our cause last year. What was it you said?"

"I said those brown uniforms reminded me of Nazi Germany in the 1930's. All that was missing was the Swastika armbands. And all who wore those uniforms were nothing but goose-stepping morons."

"Yes, you did. And do you remember what I said?"

"That one day I would regret saying those words to you."

"And that day is here, Mr. Eagle." She said "Ladies and Gentlemen, I now yield the podium to the District Overseer of the Games, Mr. Patrick McVile."

The crowd cheers and the band plays a short tune.

***

Mr. McVile took his place at the podium.

"Thank you, District Commander. Let the games begin."

The band played "We Will Rock You" one more time.

The stadium rocked as if the people were watching the Super Bowl playoff.

Holding up his hand to silence the crowd, the District Overseer turned to the people on the playing field. Before speaking he motioned to a group of security personnel standing near the goal post at the east end of the stadium. Two security guards standing about fifteen feet apart held up flags. The rest formed two columns behind the flag bearers, leaving a pathway to a gate. On the other side of the gate were buses. Buses that would soon leave to the re-education camps.

"When you hear your name called, you will step forward before the platform and make your decision to renounce your party affiliation or church denomination or not. If you renounce you will immediately head to the eastern end of the stadium" he pointed to the right "and board the buses which will transport you to the re-education camp. While in the re-education camp you will be indoctrinated in the ways of the Liberal Nationalist Party. Your progress or lack of will determine the length of your stay. If you refuse to renounce, you will go to the western end" then pointed to his left "and stand inside the smaller caged area."

The District Overseer motioned for the mayor to join him at the podium.

Startled, the mayor looked bewildered at this new turn of events. Struggling to get out of his seat he made his way to the podium. *Why am I being called? Am I being sent to the re-education camp?* Thinking to himself.

"Mr. Mayor, it will be your duty, as an obedient and faithful citizen of the Liberal Nationalist Party to call the names listed on this roster." He holds up a binder filled with 500 names. "And you will ask them three questions. First, are you or any of your family affiliated with any outlawed political party? Second, are you or any of your family members of any outlawed church denomination? Third, do you renounce your affiliation or faith in the above mentioned? You will write down their responses. Their final response will determine which direction you point them to."

Taking hold of the binder with shaky hands, the mayor approached the podium. The District Overseer leaned over and whispered into the mayor's ear "You didn't think you'd get away without dirtying your hands, did you?" Leaving the mayor, he started to take his seat. Stopping, he turned around and whispered something else to the mayor. Smiling he seated himself.

"When I call your name," croaked the mayor, "step forward in front of the podium. Adams; William, Nancy and son Billy." Croaked the mayor.

***

The District Commander exited the platform as her husband continued. Coming upon a security guard she yelled, "Bring me the Security Chief. *NOW*."

The Security Chief walked over and presented himself. "Yes, ma'am?"

"Tell me why your men did not beat down that old man?"

"We couldn't."

"What do you mean you couldn't?"

"After we beat the others down we circled the old man. But a bright light appeared around him and an invisible force prevented us from getting any closer to him. I for one was terrified by what happened. Even my men want nothing to do with the old man."

"What do you mean there was a bright light around him?"

"There was! The light shone so bright it hurt our eyes. It was as if he was being protected by God. He must be a Holy Man. Look at our faces and hands. They have been burnt after being near that old man."

"I saw nothing. There was no bright light. There was no invisible force. It was the glow from the stadium lights. Nothing more. There will be no more talk about a bright light. He is not a Holy Man and there is no God. And I don't give a damn what you or your men want. *DO YOUR JOB. YOU HEAR ME?*" Her face seemed to transform into something hideous as she shouted at him.

Fearing for his life and soul, the security chief answered "Yes, District Commander."

District Commander McVile returns to the platform and sat next to her husband. Leaning over, he whispered into her ear. She smiled.

The mayor finished reading all the names except one. Leaving the binder on the podium, he took his seat with a sigh of relief.

Stepping up to the podium the District Commander leaned over and looked at Pastor Eagle, the last man standing.

"Mr. Eagle, are you affiliated with any outlawed political party?"

"Yes, Fraulein."

"A simple yes will do. Are you a member of any outlawed church denomination?"

"Yes, Fraulein."

"Are you deliberately trying to make me mad?" she complained.

"No, Fraulein."

"Do you renounce your affiliation and faith in the above mentioned?"

"No, Fraulein."

"Damn it." She screamed. "Security, throw him into the cage."

The security chief led his team onto the field and surround the old man. As they closed in, a blinding light shone around him once more, stopping them in their tracks. They raise their hands to shield their eyes from the light. Again, an invisible force prevented them from moving closer to the old man.

A collective gasp escaped from the crowd. Even the mayor could not suppress his surprise at witnessing the bright light a second time.

THE GAMES

A deep silence fell upon the stadium.

The District Commander stared at the old man, refusing to acknowledge the presence of the bright light.

The security chief cautiously moved forward, holding his left hand out, palm open and facing the old man and points to the cage. The old man nodded and moved to the smaller cage with the security team following at a distance.

Once the old man was in the cage the security team headed back to their assigned stations. Their leader momentarily remained, looking at the old man.

There something about this old man he thought. *I can't quite put my finger on it.*

As the security chief turned to leave, the old man spoke. "God has a plan for you, Gabriel Walker. Your ancestors followed Him. Seek Him with all your heart, soul and mind and you will find your answers. Remember this, Gabriel, no matter how hard they try to exterminate the Christians there will always be a remnant." Then the old man turned to the believers and led them in singing songs of praises to the Lord God Almighty. As they sang a bright light engulfed everyone inside the cage.

The man called Gabriel was stunned. He was unnerved by the events unfolding this evening. *Who was this old man and how did he know my name? What was going on?* He wanted to know more about the old man and his strange message but his position and circumstances prevented him from staying longer. With great difficulty he returned to his command post.

***

The District Overseer made his way to the podium. Across the field, six trucks were backing up to the security fence. Local workers were busy setting up enclosed ramps between the trucks and small gates which had been welded to the security fence. Pointing to the trucks he says to the crowd "In ancient times the Romans had games where gladiators fought gladiators and Christians were fed to the lions. This evening, these Christians" pointing to the western end of the ball field "will suffer the same agony just as those misled Christians experienced so long ago. And for the non-Christians we have something special planned."

The stadium came alive. The band plays and the crowd roars.

Holding up his hand to quiet the people he continued, "Our very first sacrifice will be introduced by the District Commander." He motioned her to the podium.

"Thank you. Thank you. Now let the games continue." She said, "Security bring out Mr. Eagle."

Remembering the last encounter with the old man the two security guards moved to the smaller caged area and stopped, neither wanted to approach the gate. Finally, one of them motions for Eagle to come with them. Taking their place on either side of Eagle, yet keeping a safe distance, they continued to the center of the field. Once Eagle was in position the two guards quickly returned to the safety on the other side of the fence.

"Mr. Eagle. You are an Enemy of the State and justice will be served tonight. Do you have any last words?"

"Yes, Fraulein. Soon we will see who the real Enemy of the State is." Having said his piece, he knelt and began praying.

No longer able to contain the hatred for Eagle she screamed "Release the lions."

Workers across the field raised the gates on the truck beds and used cattle prods to move the six lions into the ramps. Angered, the lions roared and ran straight from the trucks onto the field. Once outside the lions milled about roaring and pawing at the ground. Sensing prey was close they ran to where Eagle was and circled him.

Roaring and swatting at one another they moved in closer to the sacrificial lamb.

Leaning over the podium an evil smile spread across the face of the District Commander. *I'm going to savor this moment for a long time. Justice served.* The crowd, as if on cue, rose as one to their feet and cheered.

Suddenly, a heavenly light engulfed the old man and the lions became quiet and lied down.

The crowd ceased cheering and gaped at the scene below them in bewilderment.

"Security into the cage." The District Commander screamed as she ran down the stairs. Stopping at the gate she said, "Open the gate and let's go in."

"District Commander, I recommend you wait till we have the old man."

"I will not repeat myself again. GO."

"Yes, ma'am."

Security Chief Gabriel Walker led his squad of fourteen armed men, with the District Commander, to the center of the field. When they were within twenty feet of the old man the lions became agitated and started roaring. Walker stopped his men and the lions settled back down but kept wary eyes on the intruders.

"Keep moving." Shouted the District Commander.

"We'll anger the lions and they'll attack us." Walker replied.

"Then tell your men to shoot them. Now move!"

Taking one last look at the commander Walker motioned for his men to move forward. After advancing five feet the lions jumped up and attacked.

Instinctively, Gabriel Walker knelt, dropped his

weapon and prayed. His men fired their weapons but the lions were amongst them, causing some of the men to be hit by friendly fire. The remainder tried to form a circle to better protect themselves but to no avail. The lions were too fast and powerful, the men screamed as the lions quickly ripped them apart. The screams faded into the night.

There was a collective gasp from the people.

Ignoring Gabriel Walker, the lions circled around the District Commander. They closed the gap. Looking at the old man she begs for help.

"I told you we would see who the real Enemy of the State is." He said. "May God have mercy on your soul."

"Help me!" She screamed. "Help me Patrick."

"Shoot the lions. Shoot them." Her husband shouted at security.

Rifles fire but too late. The lions lunged at Terry McVile and tore her apart until she was no longer recognizable. Her screams echoed throughout the stadium.

The crowd began screaming and crying at the horrific sight on the field. They had expected to see the old man being torn apart limb by limb and not the guards and District Commander McVile. Even the band members stood dumbfounded not knowing what to do.

Patrick McVile stood in shock after witnessing the death of his wife.

Although unnerved by the killings Mayor Morgan, seeing an opportunity, ran to the podium yelling "Get the ambulances out there. Security surround the bodies. Block the view." Turning he led Patrick McVile to one of the chairs. Returning to the microphone he said "Medical personnel to the platform."

***

THE GAMES

It took hour to bag and tag all the body parts and haul them to the morgue. The mayor approached Patrick McVile and said "Mr. McVile, our thoughts are with you on the loss of your wife. I know you're in shock at this terrible tragedy but I need to ask you what do you want to do with Mr. Eagle?"

"Huh? What?" he said, confused.

"What do we do with Mr. Eagle?"

"Eagle? Who's Eagle?"

The mayor pointed to the old man standing in the center of the football field and said "The man responsible for the death of your wife."

McVile shook his head several times as if to clear the cobwebs and turned his attention to the old man. Grabbing the arm of the mayor he yelled "I want to strangle his scrawny little neck but he deserves something much worse. Whatever happens to him will be spectacular and in front of these people. Jail him and finish off the rest." He collapsed in his chair and cried uncontrollably.

The driver pushed the mayor aside and gently led the District Overseer to the limousine. Once his employer was secured in the backseat he headed to the morgue.

The mayor approached the podium with more confidence than last time. "Ladies and gentlemen, please take your seats and prepare for the finale." The crowd sat down and many reached into the bags they brought.

"Security Chief, have the old man taken to jail and bring the rest of the prisoners to the center of the field then return to your post."

"You two! Escort the old man to the county jail." Security Chief Walker said to the same two guards who had escorted the old man from the caged area.

The two were visibly shaken when ordered to take the

old man away. Looking at each other for courage one of them finally asked "Chief, can you get someone else to take the old man? We're afraid of him."

"No," he shouted. "Now do your duty and get going."

Once on the field the prisoners, all 250, milled about wondering what was going to happen next, except for the 75 men, women and children who banded together. They knelt in a circle, prayed and gave thanks to the Lord God Almighty. The majority of the prisoners, crying and begging for mercy, could not understand how these people could remain so calm.

"Ladies and gentlemen, the time has come for your participation." Announced the mayor. "As soon as I depart the platform, the security chief will fire a flare into the air. That will be your cue to start. Remember, be careful you don't hurt the person in front of you." He hurried away.

Many in the crowd took aim at selected targets. Before anyone could fire, the 75 who refused to renounce their faith in God fell to the ground dead. Silence befell them. The shooting started and the band played 'Another One Bites the Dust.'

Prisoners run for cover but there was no place to hide. The screams and cries of agony from the wounded pierced the ears of the living. It was like shooting fish in a barrel. The crowd, who just an hour ago sat motionless and in shock at witnessing the carnage of the horrific death of the district commander and security detail, had now turned into a mob thirsting for blood hooting and hollering as bodies fell. Soon the shooting died down. Throughout the field a body moved and the crack of a rifle ended the movement. Then all was quiet.

Security Chief Walker stared in disbelief at the dead littering the field. He hadn't seen such carnage since his combat tour in Iraq.

THE GAMES

"Webber, take the guards and make sure everyone is dead." He said.

"What if any are still alive? What do we do?"

"What do you think those angry people in the stands would do if you tried to take a wounded prisoner off the field?"

"They'd probably shoot all of us."

"You have your answer." Walker said as he leaned against the fence to steady himself.

Webber and the other guards returned and confirmed all were dead from multiple gunshot wounds. He hesitated before continuing "Chief, there's something else."

"What?"

"The Christians were all dead but there were no bullet wounds on the bodies."

Walker nodded his head in acknowledgement and said "Call the clean-up crew and make sure everyone leaves the stadium before locking up."

"Aye, Chief."

Surveying the carnage on the field and hearing the laughter drifting down from the stadium Gabriel Walker said to no one in particular, "God, what have we done?"

4. LATE... AGAIN
By PAUL G BUCKNER

It began as nothing more than a soft buzzing, a vibration just on the verge of being audible. Cody ignored it. At first, anyway. Until it grew more intense, more than a simple annoyance. It was now a cacophonous roar that echoed through his head like a klaxon warning of an impending torpedo strike. Without thinking, a long thin arm snaked out of the darkness in one swift motion and silenced the alarm. He lied prone but moved again. Belly crawling, he keeps his head low. Not fast, but with purpose. The room was small, but he knew his way around. He'd studied the building plans and had been over the layout many times before. He knew where he was going.

He summoned every ounce of courage that remained. With a low, guttural groan, he threw the blankets off, sat up on the side of the bed, and steadied himself. His head felt the size of a basketball, and even though the room was pitch-black, except for the bright red alarm clock gleaming on the table next to him, his head spun like a toy windmill. A splitting, aching catastrophe made from too much tequila

LATE...AGAIN

and cigarette smoke, he made his way to the bathroom and turned on the water in the tub. A small night light above the sink told him all he needed to know when he peered into the mirror. No reason to turn on the overhead and make matters worse. He turned his attention back to the running water. It was still cold. He pulled the diverter anyway and climbed into the cold spray. The sudden arctic blast made him forget about his splitting headache, for a moment, until the water warmed and his body tempered to it. The pounding returned with enthusiasm.

The small bathroom was adequate for the thirty-two-year-old bachelor. A small stand-in shower, toilet, and vanity in a compact room painted a bright canary yellow. Not the color he would have chosen, but it was the color chosen by the previous owners of the house. A towel holder was the only thing on the wall as he wasn't one to decorate much, especially the bathroom.

Cody stepped out of the shower, towelled off and stood in front of the steamed-over mirror. He picked up the hair dryer and aimed it at the center. Within seconds the fog disappeared, and he could see his bloodshot hazel eyes staring back at him. He didn't bother using the dryer on his crew cut brown locks. It would dry enough on its own once he went outside into the heat. Besides, it wasn't like he was going out on a date this early in the morning. He shook the last of the shaving cream out of the can and made a mental note he needed to stop by the dollar store on his way home from work. He shaved the three-day stubble off his face, splashed his face with water and caught a glimpse of the alarm clock out of the corner of his eye. Five minutes past six.

"Damn! Late again," he swore. "Boss' gonna have my ass!"

He hurried to the closet, pulled on a pair of socks, his faded Levi's, and a red long-sleeved shirt before sliding his feet into his steel-toed boots. Two minutes later he was behind the wheel of his four-wheel drive, tearing down the dirt road that led to the highway.

He was late Monday because he overslept, then again on Wednesday when he went out with friends at the bar the night before. He knew he would have his butt in a ringer. He was a carpenter by trade, and had worked for the same company for over three years, but lately, he had been having a hard time getting to work on time. He glanced down at the gas gage, it was nearing empty. He pulled over at the first gas station he came to, jumped out and started the gas before running inside. He grabbed a large energy drink from the cooler and two packs of Pain-Ease for his head.

"Twenty on pump two," Cody said to the clerk while reaching for his wallet.

"That'll be $26.38 please," the clerk said.

Handing the cash to the clerk, Cody noticed he had two dollars left.

"Could I get a lottery ticket please?"

"Sure thing, buddy."

He paid for his things and hurried back to the truck. Opening both packs of the pain medicine, he threw the wrappers in the floorboard and washed them down with a large gulp of energy drink. He threw the lottery ticket in the seat next to him, among dozens of other lottery tickets that never panned out, and sped out back onto the highway.

When he arrived at the job site, the foreman never said a word, just shook his head and pointed to the office. Cody knew what that meant: he was destined for another ass-chewing. His boss, Jim Mathews, was a hard-nosed construction guy that worked hard and expected his

LATE...AGAIN

employees to work just as hard. Cody walked up the steps of the small office trailer parked on the job site and turned the knob of the aluminium door. He caught a glimpse of the work crew staring at him just before he walked in. The spring pulled the door closed behind him with a loud slam just as his boss hung up the phone. Cody winced. Not because he had interrupted his boss, but because it upset his hangover more.

"Sit down."

Cody sat in one of the two office chairs across from his boss and started to explain.

"I'm sorry, I know I'm late again, but I swear..."

"Save it, Cody. It doesn't matter. You've been late several times this month, you almost took Bill's head off the other day with that decking because you were half-asleep and you've been moody as hell. The men are fed up, I'm fed up."

Cody sat in silence, unable to look his boss in the eye. *So, this is where he's going to fire me. Damn, I need this job. If I lose it, I don't know what I'll do. I can barely pay my bills now. Did Jim get a haircut yesterday? Funny, I don't remember his hair being this short. He looks like a jackass now more than ever. Bastard! I hate his voice. Sounds like a screeching barn owl. Maybe I shouldn't have gone out last night. I didn't stay out all that late, but damn, this sucks.*

"Are you hearing me?"

"Yes sir, every word."

"This is the third time you've been late this week alone," Jim said. "I know you need the job just like everyone else. You have bills to pay, but so do I. You're responsible for you, but I'm responsible for every one of those men out there that have to cover for your ass every time you're late or call in. I'm responsible for getting this job done on time. I need someone that I can count on and we're already behind."

"Yes sir," Cody said. "I understand. I do need my job in a bad way. I swear it won't happen again."

"Five minutes late now and then, hell, even ten isn't that big of a deal, but when it's twenty and thirty minutes, and people are standing around waiting on you, it stalls the whole goddamn project. I can't have that, not on my job sites. Cody, you're fired."

"Mr. Mathews, please," he pleaded. "I really need this job. I've just had a run of bad luck this week. My truck broke down, and I had a water leak at home. Please, don't fire me. I promise it won't happen again, ever."

"You're a good hand when you're here and hooked up, but let's face it, that's rare these days. I have to have someone that I can count on."

"I know, Mr. Mathews. I promise I'll not be late again or miss a single day, I swear. I need this job."

Cody leaned forward and put on his pitiful face in hopes it would help sway his boss' decision. *Son of a bitch,* he thought. *This bastard is really firing me. This is really happening! He's damn lucky to have someone like me on this crew of misfit morons, to begin with, and this son of a bitch is seriously firing me. He's a complete idiot, no wonder he's freaking single.*

Jim leaned back in his chair, his stern look relaxing a little as he appeared in thought. "Cody," he said. "I don't know why I'm doing this, and it'll probably come back to bite me in the ass, but I'll tell you what I'm going to do. I'll let you stay on, but only on a probationary standpoint. If you're late one more time, even one minute, one second late, I'll fire your ass so fast it'll make your head spin. Got it? No exceptions."

Cody could tell by the look on the boss' face he meant every word. "Yes sir, I swear I won't."

LATE...AGAIN

"Okay, get your ass to work and don't you dare slack off."

"Yes, sir."

"Oh, and Cody?"

Cody stopped with his hand on the doorknob, looking back over his shoulder. "Yeah, boss?"

"Stick around after work tonight and clean up to make up for this morning."

Son of a bitch! Shit detail. You bastard! That's a shit job for newbies.

"Yes, sir."

***

Cody left the trailer and hurried over to the foreman.

"Get on that lift and let's get some decking up there," the foreman said.

For the next nine hours, Cody worked in the hot summer sun. His red plaid shirt, soaked with sweat and covered in dirt and grime offered little protection from the heat. He could feel his wet socks slip in his steel-toed work boots. The construction crew Cody worked for had a contract to build several high-end houses in a new development, and as Cody's boss explained earlier, they were behind. Eight-hour work days were unheard of on this crew, with the occasional exception on Fridays. Unfortunately, that was tomorrow.

When the crew knocked off for the day, Cody never felt so tired. Drained and beat. He watched everyone leave as he began cleaning up the site. An hour and a half later he settled behind the wheel of his old truck, leaving his door ajar to allow some of the hot air to escape. The last one to go for the day, it felt good that he had saved his job. He normally raced off to home to shower and change, but this week he was dead broke. He would spend the evening at home. When he checked his bank account the previous night, he had a tidy sum of $114, and a whole week to go before the next payday. He had a few credit cards, but he wasn't sure if any credit remained on any of them. *It's time to tighten the belt*, he thought. He turned the key in the ignition, but instead of starting, the truck emitted a slow clicking sound.

"Damn it!" he shouted while slamming his hands against the steering wheel. "Not the damn battery."

Dejected, he slumped back in his seat. A moment later he reached down and pulled the hood latch. There wasn't any reason for the battery to have up and died; he replaced it only last summer. Jumping out of the truck, he suddenly realized he didn't remember turning the headlights off when he parked that morning. He was in too big of a hurry. Sure enough, when he looked at the switch, it was still in the "on" position.

"Dammit," he cursed, and slammed the door. Fuming, he kicked at a rock that was unlucky enough to be near him. Everyone gone home for the day, there was no one around to give him a jump. He opened the door again and reached for his cell phone. Scrolling through his contacts, he found his friend Chris' number and hit the call button. The call went straight to voicemail.

"Chris, it's Cody. I'm broke down and need a jumpstart man. My battery is dead. Call me as soon as you get this 'cause I'm stranded."

He scrolled through his contact list to see if he could think of anyone else that may be able to help. Just as he came across another person, his phone vibrated. It was Chris.

"Hey man," Cody said. "I need your help, I'm stranded."

LATE...AGAIN

"Yeah, I got your message. Where are ya?"

"I'm at the job site. Everyone's gone home already, so I'm stuck. I guess my battery is completely dead. It was clicking earlier, but now it's not even doing that when I try it. Think you can come give me a jump?"

"Sure, but it'll be at least an hour or so. I have to pick up Katy from soccer practice and then drop her off. Are you still working on that new development over on Gibson?"

"Yeah, still here. Just turn in on the west entrance and go straight down. You'll see my truck."

When he hung up, Cody walked over to the house and sat down in the shade to wait. It was late in the evening and beginning to cool down, but it was still hot. He took his shirt off and slung it over the handle of the cement machine to dry in the wind and then lied down on the scaffolding. He nodded off a couple of times, but woke up when flies buzzed near his ears or landed on his face. An hour later he sent a text to see if his friend was close, but Chris never responded.

"Son of a bitch!" Cody shouted, kicking at a block of wood. Hot, frustrated and angry, he stood, staring into space. Walking over to the cement mixer, he pulled his now dry shirt off the handle and walked back inside. With nothing else to do but wait, he lied back down on the scaffolding and folded the shirt under his head for a pillow. Pulling his cell phone out to play on the internet awhile, he noticed the battery getting low and turned it off. He closed his eyes and soon fell asleep.

A stray dog somewhere in the night began barking and woke Cody from his nap. Sitting up in the dark, he clicked on his cell phone to see it was well past midnight. He started to text his friend again and give him a good cussing, but decided better of it when the battery light turned orange and showed less than five percent remaining. Clicking it off, he stood and made his way out to his truck using the partial moonlight as his guide. The door of the old truck creaked from rust on the weathered hinges. He jumped in and sat down. The battery was so weak the overhead light in the cab didn't come on when the door opened. Desperate, he said a silent prayer and turned the key. He knew better, but he still had to try. Slamming his hand down on the seat. he sent old papers and trash flying into the floorboard.

I've got to clean this thing out one of these days, he thought. *Where's that lottery ticket I bought this morning?* Scouring the seat in the dim light, he searched for the lottery ticket that lay among all the other failed winners, wasted money on hopes and dreams that would never come.

"There you are, come to daddy."

He flicked open his cell phone and typed in the lottery site to check his numbers. The light began to dim, so he hurried. The website came up with the evening's numbers.

12-04-41-44-25 and a Powerball number of 51.

"Wait a minute, what the hell?" He read the numbers out loud. The cell phone light dimmed, but was good enough to see the large numbers.

"WOO HOO!," he screamed. "Son of a bitch! Holy mother! No way!"

All the numbers matched. Jumping out of the pickup, he held his lottery ticket in one hand and his cell phone in the other to check one more time.

It was a match.

His cell phone shut down then, thrusting him into darkness again. It didn't matter, he was rich! In his excitement, he pounded on the hood, screaming at the top of his lungs. He could pay off his mortgage, buy a new truck, a new bass boat, a new sports car.

LATE…AGAIN

No, to hell with his mortgage. He would buy a huge house, one on the lake. It suddenly occurred to him he would never have to work again. He didn't need to worry about his job on the construction crew or working for asshole Mathews. He never did like the son of a bitch anyway. He couldn't wait to tell the bastard to kiss his ass. Morning couldn't arrive fast enough.

***

It was late, or early, he couldn't tell which anymore, but it was well after dark and Cody's stomach growled. It was miles to the highway no matter which direction he walked. He knew if he took off walking in one direction, his friend would show up from a different direction and miss each other entirely. No, he had to stay put. He turned on a small radio the men used during the work day and laid back on the scaffolding.

Too excited to sleep, he couldn't sit still. He headed back out to his truck and tried the engine one more time, but it was no use. The overhead light glowed a soft, dim yellow. He slumped back in the driver's seat and closed his eyes.

***

A car door slammed nearby and Cody woke with a start.

"You're here early," Jim Mathews said, walking to the trailer. "Good, about damn time!"

"What?" Cody sat up in his seat, rubbing his eyes.

He had fallen asleep waiting for his friend that never showed. After a few seconds, he shook the cobwebs loose and realize what happened. The rest of the crew had arrived and were heading to the job site to start the day.

Cody grabbed for his shirt pocket and sighed with relief when he pulled the lottery ticket out. He shoved it back in his pocket when one of his buddies pulled in beside him.

"Hey Sammy, you got any jumper cables? My battery is completely dead."

"What? You mean for after work today?"

"No, I mean right now," Cody said, grinning. "I'm leaving, I'm out of here, for good."

"Mathews fire you?"

"Oh hell no. He can't afford to lose me, but I'm quitting. I'll tell you why as soon as I get my truck going. So you got any cables or not?"

"Yeah, sure."

Sammy ambled over to his truck, retrieved the cables and got Cody's truck started in no time. They took the cables off and slammed the hood.

"Thanks, Sammy."

"Sure, now mind telling me what the hell's going on?"

Cody grinned and walked back to his truck, got in and drove up to the office door where he parked and laid into the horn. It didn't take long before everyone stood around to see what all the commotion was about.

Jim Mathews threw the office door open and stepped out. "What the hell are you doing, you idiot? Shut that damn thing off and quit honking that goddamn horn."

Cody got out of his truck and jumped onto the hood.

"Now that I have your attention, I am hereby informing you of my resignation," Cody shouted, pulling the lottery ticket from his shirt pocket. "You are now looking at the latest millionaire in the fine state of Oklahoma." Waving the ticket around, he looked right at his boss. "Mr. Mathews, you can officially kiss my ass. I quit!"

LATE...AGAIN

"What the hell are you blabbering about?" a voice came from the crowd.

"I won the lottery. My numbers came up, you sorry sonsabitches. I won't forget ya'll though. After I collect my winnings, I'll be back and give all of ya'll a little *walking-around* money to fill your pockets. I might even buy you that new forklift that Mathews here is too tight to get you!"

By this time all the men gathered around. Some laughed at him, probably because they thought he was either drunk or on drugs.

Cody jumped off the pickup, climbed in behind the wheel and peeled out of the driveway, flinging dirt and gravel high into the air as he shouted and waved out the window.

"You damn fool," Matthews shouted. "Don't let me catch you around one of my job sites again! Get back to work everyone."

Cody drove as fast as he dared down the dirt road. When he reached the highway, it occurred to him he didn't know where he was going. He won a few dollars here and there with scratch offs, but he was able to cash his winning tickets in at the same little store by his house. Surely they knew what he needed to do and where to go. He would stop there and ask.

Ten minutes later, he slammed the door on his truck and ran inside. The clerk was busy with a customer, but Cody couldn't wait.

"Hey man, where do I go if I've won the lottery? Is there like an official headquarters or something?"

The clerk looked up at the same time the customer turned around to see who was shouting.

"Be right with you," the clerk said. He handed the customer back her change.

"Now, what's your question?"

Cody pulled out his lottery ticket and held it aloft. "I've won the lottery! Where do I go to get my money?"

"Impossible. You couldn't have won it."

"Right here's my numbers, I'll read 'em off to you. 12-04-41-44-25, and 51 by god!"

"Well, that's the winning numbers alright," the clerk said. "But I never heard there was a winner. The jackpot went up to one-hundred and twelve million."

"What? That can't be right. Right here's my ticket, and all the numbers match."

Several customers had crowded around out of curiosity.

"Can I see that ticket?"

Cody, leery of handing his fortune over to a complete stranger was more than a bit nervous, but he figured with all the people standing around as witnesses he had nothing to lose. He handed it to the clerk, who carefully examined it. Cody waited, his heart racing. He knew the clerk would confirm it once he matched up the numbers.

The man looked up and handed it back laughing.

"Sorry, bud, these are the correct numbers for last night's drawing alright, no doubt about it," the clerk chuckled. "But this ticket was for the drawing two weeks ago!"

5. LORD WILLING AND THE CREEK DON'T RISE

By MARK COOK

The cold steel of the shotgun barrel rattles against my teeth as I try to control my trembling hands. With tear-filled eyes, I say a silent goodbye to my wife, Carol, and my two girls. I have rehearsed this so many times in my head. It is so much easier when the gun isn't pressing against the roof of my mouth. My index finger slowly squeezes the trigger. I know my pain will soon be over forever. Just as the shotgun should have fired, a horn sounds and I hear a familiar voice.

"Hello! Is anyone there? Hello?" I jerk the gun barrel from my mouth and wipe the saliva off my chin with my shirtsleeve. I stand on wobbly legs and walk to the front window. A primer patched Chevy truck is parked in the dirt driveway. With both ends higher than the crushed middle, the rusted bumper seems to smile at me. A lightning bolt crack crosses the entire windshield from right to left. A tall, skinny man steps out of the truck and walks up the cracked cement sidewalk. Well, I'll be damned. I walk to the door and out onto the front porch.

"Hey don't shoot, I'm friendly," calls the voice. I forgot I still have the shotgun in my hands. I turn and lean it up against the wall of the house.

"Is that you Matt?" He says with a full tooth grin. "Well, I'll be! It is you!"

"Hi Billy. How are you?" Billy Walker was my best friend growing up. I haven't seen him since I moved away. Billy pumps my hand and grins at me with a mouth too small to hold his enormous pearly white teeth. "Come take a load off," I say. I want him to leave, but nothing would be gained by being rude. I ease into the old redwood rocking chair. There isn't a chair for Billy to lighten his load, so he leans against a battleship blue paint-chipped support post.

"I thought that was you. I seen that truck and just knew it had to be you!" Billy is the kind of person who would give you everything he had if you needed it. He would never survive in the city.

"What are you doing these days, Billy?" Really I am interested in is taking care of some unfinished business.

"Oh, you know, this and that. Whatever I can do to put food on the table. Mostly I just do odd jobs and help around Old Lady Hitchcock's store."

"You mean she trusts you after what you did to her rooster?" I laugh.

When I was ten and Billy was twelve, we used to spend our free time trying to get into as much mischief as possible. Actually, it didn't start out that way. We were just bored and needed something to do. Our favorite pastime was to take our B.B. guns and sneak over to Old Lady Hitchcock's place. Her chicken house backed up to the woods, which gave us the perfect opportunity to lie in wait and take pot shots at her chickens. We didn't try to kill the chickens. We just liked to shoot them in the tail end and watch them hop around like three-legged frogs in a frying pan.

On one of these shooting expeditions, Billy shot Old Lady Hitchcock's prize rooster right in its beady little eye. It was an accident. But accident or not, that red and black plumed rooster was dead. Unfortunately, Mrs. Hitchcock chose that moment to walk around the corner of the chicken house, and she saw us shoot her precious old rooster.

Billy and I took off running as fast as our legs would go. We ran all the way to Grandma's house and hid in the root cellar until we thought it was safe to come out. Grandma must have known we were down there because when we opened the creaky cellar door and stepped out into the sunlight, she and Old Lady Hitchcock were standing there, Grandma with a switch and Old Lady Hitchcock armed with the dead rooster. Both of them started pounding us on the back and head. Feathers flew everywhere, and Billy and I were screaming bloody murder. After we took our licking, Grandma made us apologize to Old Lady Hitchcock and then sent Billy home to face the wrath of his folks.

"I guess she forgot about my criminal past when she hired me. The old girl died a few years back. I'm workin' for her daughter now," Billy says laughing.

"I hope she doesn't swing a rooster as hard as her mom," I chuckle and then nearly double over in pain. I grab my stomach as sharp bolts of fire shoot through my intestines and seem to ricochet off each rib. The doctors took half my stomach out trying to cut away the cancer that was slowly eating away my insides.

"You all right? You don't look so good."

LORD WILLING AND THE CREEK DON'T RISE

"I'll be okay in a minute. It only lasts a few minutes at a time," I say gritting what's left of my teeth. The pain seems to last longer each time. Billy nods his head, and I can tell he feels uncomfortable watching me writhe in pain. Billy looks at me like he is seeing me for the first time. I can only imagine what he thinks as he stands, staring at what was once a vibrant man, but is now a walking scarecrow. The chemo and radiation therapy weakened my teeth causing some of them to fall out. With the teeth gone, my cheeks sink inward. What was once a full head of dark black hair is now only a memory. My strong body surrendered to the disease and now is little more than a skeleton that can barely hold up my pants and shirt.

"I heard you had cancer," he says.

"Stomach cancer," I say uncomfortably. I don't want everyone knowing my problems. I stare across the hay meadow across the road. The early morning sun is still trying to peek through the thick fog that covers the valley. To the east, nearly invisible, Eldon Mountain stands like a guardian over the gray valley.

Billy studies me for a few more moments and then looks over at my old shotgun leaning by the door. "You goin' huntin'?" he asks, seeming to already know the answer.

"No," I say, tiring of our visit and not wanting to admit the reason for the gun.

We sit in silence once again. Billy seems to be trying to find the right words.

"You wanna talk about it? I'm a purty good listener."

"There's nothing left to say. Why don't you leave now?" I say with more animosity than I mean.

Billy stares at me, and I can tell I hurt him. He jerks away from the post he is leaning on and with what seems like only a few strides of his long, gangly legs, is back to his truck. He turns and faces me. Staring me in the eyes, he asks, "Why did you come back here?" I stare back but can't answer him. Billy jumps in the truck and slams the door. Gravel shoots out from beneath his rear tires as he floors the accelerator and fishtails out of the driveway. My eyes follow the dust cloud all the way to the highway. Then all traces of Billy are gone except for his lingering question, "Why did you come back here?"

This was my grandparents' home. My father was born here and his father before him. My grandparents passed away over ten years ago, leaving me the farm. I haven't been back to the place since their funeral. This place is too full of memories, good and bad. The bad is stronger than the good.

From the looks of this place, no one has been here during that time, and Mother Nature hasn't been kind.

The old wooden gate that stood sentry for so many years is now white with age and clings to the corner post by a single hinge. The chicken wire fence, which never served any purpose known to me, now lies along the ground. Crabgrass weaves in between the wire making it nearly impossible to move, even if one so desired. The old swing set sits idle, more rust showing than paint. There are no children to enjoy it. No one to slide down the aluminum slide. No children on the swing laughing and hollering, "push me higher, weeeee", only memories.

With Billy gone I lose the courage to finish my self-destruction and walk back in the house. The front room looks the same, almost as if Grandma and Grandpa still live here. Their recliners still sit in the corner, with an end table sitting between them like a referee. The old fireplace is full of ashes, and mouse droppings are scattered across the yellowing tile floor. I take a few steps toward the kitchen before another stomach spasm changes my mind and

LORD WILLING AND THE CREEK DON'T RISE

knocks me to the floor. I tuck myself in a fetal position and pray for the pain to end. Once again God ignores me.

Five minutes later the pain subsides enough for me to uncurl and slide across the mouse droppings to my Grandma's recliner. Using the last of my energy, I grip the armrest and pull myself into the chair. The pain seems to be ebbing. I push the chair into a fully reclined position and close my eyes.

"Damn you, God!" I scream to the empty room. "What did I do to deserve this?" I slam my fist down on the armrest. A cloud of dust rises from the chair as pain shoots up my arm all the way to my shoulder. A creamy, white porcelain cat falls off the end table, shattering as it hits the floor. That was my Grandma's favorite cat. I gave it to her for Mother's Day when I was about ten years old. I ease myself over the arm of the chair and pick up the small pieces.

Stretching to pick up the head of the cat, I find a cardboard box underneath the end table. The lid is labeled "Important Papers" in Grandma's finest chicken scratch. Inside I find old, faded family pictures and yellowing report cards from my dad's school days. I find a picture of my wife Carol taken when we were eight years old. We grew up together and always knew we would spend the rest of our lives as one. In the picture, her long, graceful legs were hidden underneath a pair of Big Smith overalls. Her corn-silk hair was pulled back into a ponytail.

Pressed against the side of the box is a newspaper clipping. The newspaper is the Cherokee Herald, dated June 19, 1975. The headline reads Former State Trooper Commits Suicide. "This can't be!" I mumble to myself. "This can't be." Shocked and bewildered, I begin to read the article. It said my father, Roy Owens, had been fighting a losing battle with cancer and local police officials felt that is why he killed himself.

My grandparents told my sister and me that my dad died from the cancer.

I close my eyes and try to remember the days before and after my dad's death. A few months before my father's death, my family moved back to the farm so Granny could help my dad recover from surgery. Supposedly the surgery to remove the grapefruit-sized tumor had been successful; at least that's what my sister, Casey, and I were told. We were ready for Daddy to recover so we could get on with the rest of our lives.

His bedroom was near the front of the house, and that's where he spent all of his time. He was so weak from chemotherapy and so drugged with painkillers that some days he couldn't move his arms and legs or even speak. On those days, the only indication that he heard you or even recognized you was by the rapid blinking in his glassy eyes. Even my father's favorite spot, the front porch, was off limits because they couldn't get the bed out the front door without taking it apart. So Daddy spent his last days staring for hours out the bedroom window.

Days before Daddy's death, I was afraid to go visit him. I knew seeing his emaciated, skeleton-like body and his dazed expressions would make me confront the obvious, so I chose not to say goodbye to the man helped me into this world. That cowardly decision still haunts me. I wish I had been brave enough to hold his frail hand and tell him how much I loved him and how much he meant to me. Instead, I chose to play behind the house or spend almost all of my time over at a friend's house, out of sight, but never out of mind. I was a coward when courage was needed the most.

A noise on the front porch brings my mind back to the old empty house. "Who's there?" I holler. No one

LORD WILLING AND THE CREEK DON'T RISE

answers. I hear more noises, but again no one answers my call. A lack of energy supersedes my curiosity. It's probably the wind or just the house settling I tell myself. I pick up the newspaper and read the last paragraph. It said the funeral would be at Reed-Culver Funeral Home on Wednesday.

God, the funeral. How I hated that day. The overpowering smell of sweet flowers, the parlor so packed people were standing against the wall in the back. Policemen, in their dress uniforms with black armbands, were there from all over the state. I had never met most of them, but they all knew and respected my father. Daddy's favorite saying was "Lord willing and the creek don't rise". The creek rose one last time.

The ceremony was a typical Southern Baptist ritual. The choir sang "Shall We Gather at the River" badly while I sat numbly on a hard wooden bench near the front, trying to be brave and not cry. I think the ceremony was the hardest on Granny because she had cared for him during the last few months. She watched him die a little every day. Granny did her best not to break down in front of everyone, but it still happened. No one could fault her. A mother has a right to grieve for a lost child, especially one taken in his prime and in such a horrible way.

I managed pretty well until the preacher opened the casket so people could view the body. I looked into the casket and lost all control. That wasn't my father! My dad was heavy from years of overindulging in his favorite foods. This person was wafer thin and alien-like. I wanted to scream, "That's not my dad!" But it was him. I couldn't wait to get out of there. I didn't have the guts to say goodbye to him when he was alive, and I sure couldn't face up to this now that he was dead.

I have been trying to forget that day for 25 years. I

begin weeping. It starts out with just a few tears, turns into a wailing from deep inside my soul and ends with screams and curses aimed at the Lord Almighty. The Lord who takes a small boy's mother before she can experience his first birthday. The Lord who takes a 12 year-old boy's father before he can see his son become a man. The Lord willing to take what is most precious and destroy it with a whim. The Lord willing to kill me in the same way.

I collect myself and dry my eyes with a dusty Kleenex from the box on the end table. My grandparents' lies still hang heavy on my heart, but I understand why they did what they did. It was much easier for Casey and me to think that cancer had murdered our father rather than him killing himself like I intend to do.

My stomach rumbles. I look at my watch and find that it is nearly noon. The whole morning has disappeared into an anthology of bad memories. When I arrived here early this morning, I hadn't planned on being in this world for much longer, so I didn't bother packing a lunch. Now hunger pains are reminding me that not only did I skip breakfast this morning, but dinner last night as well. I ease myself out of the recliner and walk sluggishly into the kitchen, gently placing one foot in front of the other. I am afraid if I fall, I will not have the energy to get back up. The cabinet doors are all open, and the countertops are thick with dust. The pantry is empty. What memories this place holds.

I could see Granny, her timeworn face singing "He Set Me Free". Her calloused hands reaching over the hot burners on the stove to stir the creamy white gravy. I watch her reach into the oven and pull out one of her melt-in-your-mouth apple pies; the flaky, golden crust with tart Jonathan apples covered in cinnamon tempt even the strongest willpower. And oh those made-from-scratch biscuits, dripping in homemade strawberry preserves or sweet golden honey. If ever there were heaven on earth, it would be in Granny's kitchen.

My protesting stomach brings me back to the present. Since the operation that removed most of my stomach and intestines, I survive mainly on liquids; anything solid usually comes back up. What I wouldn't give to be able to eat Grandma's cooking again.

With no hope of satisfying my hunger, I walk out of the house to the front porch. The sun has finally burned through the morning fog and hangs high in the bright sky, puffy white balls of cotton drift without a care. As a famous Indian once said, "Today is a good day to die."

Down below the house is the creek I played in during my childhood. I grab the shotgun and hobble toward a place of happy memories. When I get to the bank of the little creek, I find the spring rains have nearly doubled its size. A swift current throws limbs against the bank and then changes its mind and pulls them back. I sit down under a huge oak tree, the shotgun at my side, and let my body relax.

On the bank just down from where I sit, two mockingbirds gossip about the unscrupulous blue jay who torments everything in its path by darting down and screaming insults. Above my head, two gray squirrels, still skinny from the long winter, fight over the sweet-smelling acorns that adorn the stalwart oak I use as my backrest.

Downstream, where the sun sneaks in between the thick canopy of sycamore trees, coal black dairy cows chew on rich green weeds. Watching the cows mesmerizes me. First, they rip the succulent, moist weeds from the rich dirt and then with their mouths set on tumble-dry, they roll it in their cuds for what seems like hours. They never swallow, just chew and roll…chew and roll…chew and roll.

A stomach spasm doubles me over and causes me to spit up blood and kiss the rich Oklahoma dirt. The dark red blood contrasts with the rich green fescue grass. The spasm lasts for about ten minutes, causing me to roll around on the ground with knees to chin. The doctors want me to take morphine. I refuse. I will not live my last few months in a daze like Daddy did.

I can't stand it anymore. As soon as the spasm eases, I pick up the shotgun. I shove the cold steel barrel into my mouth and pull the trigger. Nothing happens. I move the selector to the bottom barrel and pull the trigger. Nothing happens. As sweat trickles down my bony face, I break open the barrel of the over-and-under and check the chambers. Both are empty.

"You lookin' for these?" a voice calls from across the creek. I squint my eyes and see Billy standing in the shadows. In his hands are two shotgun shells. I stand, using the shotgun to steady myself, and start to cross the creek. The water is too swift. Even a strong swimmer would have a difficult time reaching the far bank, much less an invalid like me.

"How did you get those?" I scream across the creek.

"Took 'em while you was in the house," he drawls.

I guess it wasn't the house creaking after all. "Throw them here. You had no right to take 'em."

"Just like you got no right to kill yourself and leave your family hurtin'."

"I have to. I can't go on living in this pain. I can't go on spitting up blood and wishing to God I was dead. Can't you see that? I don't want Carol and the kids to see me waste away a little bit every day until I'm a skeleton like my dad was. You saw my dad. Remember what he looked like before he died?"

"I remember. I also remember you sayin' somethin'

about not saying goodbye to your daddy. How will your kids' feel when they find out they didn't get to say goodbye to their daddy? How is Casey going to feel when her brother blows his brains out? You're the only family she's got left. I was your best friend growin' up, and you weren't even going to bother to say goodbye to me. You know what your problem is? You don't have the balls to face up to your problems."

Everything Billy was saying was the truth, but it still infuriated me. "Did you know my dad killed himself? Did you know this whole time and never bothered to tell me?"

"I knew about it as soon as it happened. My folks told me not to tell you. They thought it was best if you was told after you'd grown up some more." Billy looked down at his feet, shifting his weight from one leg to the other. I could tell he was bothered by the decision.

"I would have told you if your dad killed himself."

"Maybe you would have, but it wasn't my decision to make. Your granny and grandpa told my folks that you and Casey was too young to know. My folks and I just followed their wishes. I wanted to tell you, and that's the God's honest truth. But by the time I got up the courage to talk to you about it, you'd moved away."

"Give me the shells," I said crying.

"Kiss my ass. Come get 'em if you want 'em. Just remember. Your kids have the right to see their daddy 'fore he dies. You chose not to see your daddy and look what it done to you. My God, you and Carol have known each other forever. You played together right here in this creek when you was kids. Don't you care about what she wants?"

"Just give me the shells. It's my life."

"Fine you want the shells you selfish fool, I'll give 'em to you!" Billy throws the shells. They land on my side of the shiny white flint rock bank. "Kill yourself! Who gives a damn!" Billy turns his back on me and disappears into the shadows.

I reach down to pick up the shells. My leg collapses in a spasm, sending me into the swift, frigid water. I try to scream, but when I open my mouth water fills it. I wave my arms trying to turn over, but the water keeps pushing and shoving me into rocks and tree limbs. Visions of Carol and the kids flash through my mind: Sunday afternoons playing on the jungle gym; my girls laughing and shrieking, sweat pasting their long golden hair to their red cherubic cheeks; sweet innocent Carol, beautiful inside and out, grabbing my St. Louis Cardinals' hat and running for the pond. I give chase threatening to throw her in after the old hat.

A log crashing into my ribs jerks my mind back to reality. As I bob up and down along the creek, crashing into debris under the water, I see Billy walking along the bank oblivious to me. I try to call out, but my mouth fills with water. Around the approaching bend, I see what is left of a beaver dam. I angle toward it and exhausting my last ounce of strength manage to wrap my arms around a thick log. "Billy! Billy! Help! Help me!" I scream hoping Billy can hear me over the crashing water. I jerk my head all around. Where's Billy? He's gone. I am shivering so badly that I can barely grip the log.

The aggressive current finally steals the last of my strength and sends me spinning down the creek. My head goes under the water. I relax and let the water carry me away. A calming light blankets my goose-bumped body with warmth. Then something starts pulling me backwards, away from the light, away from my warm cocoon. I feel myself leave the swift current of the creek. A voice hollers for me to open my eyes. I want to holler

LORD WILLING AND THE CREEK DON'T RISE

back "they are open", but my mouth won't move.

"Open your eyes, Matt. Stay with me."

My body starts shaking like a dog fresh out of the bathtub. I can make out the outline of someone standing above me. "Billy?"

"It's me, Matt. Thank God you're okay," he says as he takes off his jacket and wraps it around my shoulders. I sit there for five minutes trying to will my teeth to stop chattering. Finally, my teeth stop pounding together and I scream at Billy. "You stupid jerk! You almost caused me to drown!" I call Billy every profane word I can think of and even make up a few more. He never says a word. When I stop cussing, mainly due to a lack of air, Billy walks over to me and sits down.

"For a man who wants to die you sure was fightin' to stay alive," Billy says with a sly smile on his face.

I stare at him and try to come back with something. I fail. He is right. I do want to live. I want to see my wife. I want to tell her how much I love her. I want to hold my kids again.

"Help me back to my truck. I have some people to see."

"That's what I wanted to hear," Billy says smiling. He grabs me underneath my arms and helps me to my feet. With Billy's help, I make it back up the hill and to my truck. Billy pulls an old, tattered blanket from behind his truck seat and wraps it around my shriveled body. I open the door to the truck , start it and turn on the heater full blast. After a few minutes, I feel blood returning to my tingling hands and feet.

Billy comes back shortly holding the old newspaper clipping. "Thought you might want this."

"No I don't think so," I say as I step out of the truck. "Thanks for all your help. I just have one question, though. How did you know I was going to be here?"

Billy crawls into his truck. When he turns back to face me, he is smiling from ear to ear. Billy gives me a Cub Scout salute and slams his foot down on the accelerator, Goodyear tires spitting gravel twenty feet behind them. That is when I remember I still have his blanket. I wave at him to stop, but his truck disappears into a cloud of thick brown dust. Maybe he'll stop at Hitchcock's store, and I can catch him there.

I take one last look at the house as I ease out on to the dirt road. Soon a cloud of dust is chasing me down the road and keeps me from taking another look at the house through the rear view mirror.

I stop at Hitchcock's store to buy a Dr. Pepper. When I come out, an old timer is sitting on the front steps.

"Excuse me, sir," I say easing by him. "Have you seen Billy come through here?"

"Billy who?" the old man looks up at me, a puzzled expression on his weather etched face.

"Billy Walker," I say.

"Billy Walker you say?"

"That's right. Billy just saved my bacon when I fell in the creek. I have his blanket in my truck, and I need to get it back to him."

"That's gonna be pretty hard to do." He says staring hard at me through milky blue eyes. "Billy Walker died in a car wreck two days ago."

I stand there dumbfounded. Thousands of neurotransmitters suddenly came to a standstill. I have many questions but only one comes out of my mouth. "Where did it happen?"

The old man pulls out his pocket knife and cuts off a chunk of apple. "Up on Eldon Mountain. Just look for the telephone pole all bent over. That's what Billy hit."

LORD WILLING AND THE CREEK DON'T RISE

I thank him and get in the truck. I take a long pull on the Dr. Pepper and immediately regret it. Branding irons shoot through my stomach. For a second the pain is so intense I think I will pass out. The pain finally becomes tolerable and I start the truck and drive up Eldon Mountain.

The first thing I see is skid marks on the pavement. About twenty yards off the road I see the bent over pole. I ease the truck off the road and park. I walk towards the pole and stop. Not ten yards into the woods stands a doe and her two fawns. I stand statue still. The doe walks over to the pole and stops. The fawns follow only a few feet behind. I guess they are a good reason for the skid marks on the road. "Looks like we both owe Billy our lives."

6. MY NAME IS EMMA
By AARIKA COPELAND

For Zoii
Because you asked

The Arizona heat weighs on me like a wool blanket. Cacti replace the trees I'm used to, wisps of leftover clouds from far away drift through the pale blue sky, and the dry heat breaks out beads of sweat across my temples. I feel like I might float away. Up, up into the sky, my lungs full of hot air.

I pull out my Percy Jackson water bottle and take two big gulps.

I'm starting to feel like a toasted marshmallow. My insides feel mushy, while my skin is crispy with a new sunburn.

Two other kids wait at the bus stop with me. A girl no older than seven swings around the stop sign pole, her pigtails flying behind her. The boy sitting on the curb is a high schooler. His ears are plugged with headphones, while his thumbs fly over the keyboard on his phone.

I've been riding this bus for two weeks. And neither of them has said more than 'hey' to me. Nothing new. It is never easy making friends when I am always the new girl. Everyone already has the friends they want.

Why would they need a new one?

The bus comes to a squeaking halt in front of us, and the doors slide open. The teenager rises with all the eagerness of a sloth. The younger girl is first in line, then the boy. By the time I plant my feet on the first step, the doors slam shut behind me, the driver is off, and I'm left to stumble the rest of the way.

The elementary girl squeals with her group of friends, their noses deep in a J-14 magazine. The boy slouches in a seat near the middle, his arm dangling around the shoulder of a girl who whispers in his ear.

I scan for a place to sit. Ah, there. The very back.

Girls snicker, and boys stare as I maneuver through the jungle of loose legs and randomly placed backpacks.

The driver swerves around cars like a snake around rocks, and I sway against the movements.

Finally, the back seat. Great! The cushion hangs off the hinges. I plop down and lean against the chair while pulling my oversized bag into my chest.

A big bump causes my glasses to slip down my nose and onto the floor. A boy in the seat to my right picks them up.

"You want me to throw them out?" he taunts. He dangles them from his thumb and forefinger near the open window. "Maybe your parents will let you pick out your own. Some that aren't so ugly?" He scrunches his nose as he says the last word.

"I picked those out myself!" I say, jumping up and

reaching for my glasses.

He tosses them at me. Two boys from the seat in front of him watch over the edge of the brown cushioned bus seat and let out a laugh before rolling their eyes and turning around to sink back into their conversation. I push the black, full circle glasses back up my nose and squat down against the broken seat. I open my bag and dig around until my hand feels a spine. I pull out a book.

My mother doesn't understand why I carry so many.

"You should take some out," she said this morning, seeing my lopsided stance.

What she doesn't know is that my books are better than most of the kids at the schools. These books are my friends.

I trace the letters on the front cover, something I always do. Dressed in white furs and sitting on an icy throne is the witch. She wears a crown of ice. She turns to me and says, "You needn't finish the story, darling. Things are perfect here. Wouldn't you enjoy some Turkish delight, instead?"

In her outstretched hand is a sweet powdered treat that waters my mouth, but I remember how tricky the white witch can be and quickly open the book, bending the front cover and squashing it against the back.

As I read, the air around me cools. The sounds of laughter shrink away. The black ink of printed words turns white, while frost creeps along the corners of the pages. Snow tickles the tip of my nose.

The bus lurches over a bump in the road. When it lands, the air is no longer stale and hot, but crisp and cold. And I am no longer leaning against an old, sagging seat, but riding the back of a giant lion. The lion's fur is warm and soft. His enormous paws stir up flurries as they hit the ground in stride. I dig my face into his mane and hug him tight.

"Hold on little one," he growls.

I can hear birds chirping their morning songs. Flowers bloom around us, and the musky smell of bark and moss lingers in the air. The snow beneath us begins to melt the further we run. Winter turns to spring before our eyes.

The lion slows to a trot before stopping completely. "Time to get off!"

"No, not yet," I plead. I want him to keep going.

"Hello!" an unfamiliar voice complains. "I said time to get off my bus."

I look up.

The driver waves his arms. I jump up when I notice I'm the last on the bus.

"Kids today," he mumbles as I pass him.

A swarming mass of kids circles the main building like bees to their hive.

They scramble when the bell rings, and I'm caught in their torrent and swept along into the school.

I sit between two girls during first hour. It's hard not to notice their double-ear piercings or that they can wear eyeshadow and lipstick to school. They don't talk to me; they just use me to pass notes back and forth to each other.

Today is like every other, except that Mrs. Garoutte catches me handing one of the notes to Alex, the girl sitting to my right.

She snatches the note out of my hand. "What's this? Is it important enough that it needs to interrupt my math lesson?"

I feel the eyes of the whole class on me, and I wish I had an invisibility cloak.

"Let's find out what is so important," she says as she undoes the elaborately folded note.

She clears her throat and reads the note aloud. "Robby

is super cute. I think he likes me. Do you think I should talk to him?"

The class erupts in giggles.

Oh no! My eyes widen, and my face grows hot as coals. "N-No!" I stammer. "That's not mine."

"Save it, Miss Jones. Do not interrupt my class again."

My cheeks burn, and against my determination, my eyes water with tears. I know I must look pathetic. I don't even know Robby.

Mrs. Garoutte hands the note to a boy in the back row. He turns his auburn head and looks at me with his honey colored eyes. He gives a half smile before looking down at his math book. I die a little inside.

The lunch bell is a huge relief. I want to get away from Robby, and all the other snickering kids.

It's bad enough to be known as the book nerd; adding stalker freak will not help.

I wait in the lunch line. Mom refused to let me bring my lunch again. She says this way I can't find a corner to hide in. That I'll have to find a seat next to someone, and that will lead to talking, and that will lead to new friends.

Yeah, right.

Today is pizza day, and more kids eat from the cafeteria than usual.

Boys shout as they toss around a football. I see the ball fly in the air, zooming straight toward me. One of the boys smashes into me in attempt to catch it and my bag slips off my shoulder.

Books fly out and scatter all around the floor. The boy shrugs before offering a quick 'sorry,' then runs off to his friends.

No one helps me. A few people laugh. And by the time I have my books safely tucked into their rightful place, I am no longer looking forward to pizza.

MY NAME IS EMMA

I find the library.

Clusters of chairs make up the back corner, next to a long window that overlooks a few trees in the parking lot. I set my backpack down in one of the chairs and sink into another.

I wish we were back in Oklahoma. At least there I had Lizzy. She and I were partners for a book report, and she liked how excited I was about the project. She invited me to a sleepover, and we had been close ever since.

Until we moved to the desert.

It's the third time we've moved in the last four years. Mom says, "Your dad goes where they tell him." But I am tired of moving from school to school. I've tried making friends here, but I'm the word nerd no one speaks to, just like the last school.

No one has even asked for my name.

I take a deep breath and remind myself I have friends right here.

The satchel swallows my arm as I fish for a new adventure. I catch one and pull it out.

As my finger glides over the bends in the letters, they begin to glow. They grow brighter and brighter until I'm forced to blink against the golden shine.

When I open my eyes, Violet Baudelaire stands in front of me, handing me a ribbon.

"Quick, tie your hair."

I grab the ribbon and form a bow at the base of my neck.

"We need something to strain these noodles," Klaus says from behind me. "Sunny, I need you to open this can, please." He hands the baby at his feet a can of tomato sauce.

Sunlight filters through the water stained window, showcasing layers of dust and cobwebs around the kitchen in a pale haze. I check inside cabinets and pull out drawers. No sign of a strainer. Wait. I pull the mesh frame out of the window and hold it up to Klaus.

"Will this do?" I ask.

"Perfect."

Klaus snatches the frame and lowers it into the kitchen sink before pouring a pot of boiling noodles over it. "Lunch is over," he says.

"What?" I say. "We haven't finished making it yet."

"Lunch is over."

The librarian is standing in front of me. She has one hand on her hip.

"Oh. Sorry." I grab my bag and hurry to my next class.

The end of the day is finally here, and I'm going to ask mom if she will homeschool me when she picks me up.

I wait on the sidewalk for her blue Jeep. Students occupy most of the benches, so I stand. I might as well make the end of the school day the best part: I pull out my favorite book.

I'm only a few pages in when a book lands with a thud at my feet. Instinctively, I kneel down to pick it up, and to my surprise, it's the same novel in my hand.

Harry Potter.

Standing, I look up to find the person who has dropped it.

My insides flip when I come face to face with the boy from first hour.

A smile spreads across his face, and the hint of a blush flushes his cheeks.

I begin stumbling over my words, trying to get them out.

"I-I didn't write that not," I finally blurt.

He laughs. "I didn't think you did. I notice your kind of the filling in the middle of those two cookies."

MY NAME IS EMMA

I hand him his book. "I like your glasses," he says.

"Oh. Thanks. I picked them out myself." I push them further up my nose.

"You like HP?"

"Yeah. I'm working my way through the whole series again."

I cringe inside and curse myself. If he doesn't already think I'm a book nerd, he does now.

"Yeah, me too."

I smile, showing all my teeth.

A horn blares across the parking lot. "That's me," he says. "Gotta go."

He moves to leave but turns back. "I'm Robby by the way."

I don't wait for the question. "My name is Emma."

Robby waves, then jogs across the parking lot toward a silver truck.

I'm still smiling when mom's Jeep squeaks to a stop in front of me.

7. NIGHT CREATURE
By JOHN D KETCHER JR

Screech. Screech.

Came the sound of the steel manhole cover slowly coming off the entrance leading to the storm drain. Strange creatures live in the miles of tunnels underneath the town of P. Creek. Slender claws appear out of the manhole, followed by a slinky, slimy and foul smelling creature.

The night creature.

Once out, the creature takes a moment to stretch the black, snake-like body to its full height of seven feet. The night creature only comes out after the sun goes down to hunt for food. Dogs, cats, wild animals. Anything easy to take into the tunnels.

The night creature, while roaming the alleyways, often hears the cries of children who have suffered at the hands of grown-ups. When it hears children crying it reaches out and gives comfort, just as a lioness sometimes gives comfort to a young impala after its mother has been killed. Knowing this scares the children, the night creature stays out of sight while seeking children living in fear.

NIGHT CREATURE

Looking around, the night creature ponders upon which direction to go. Then it hears the wail of sirens from far off, coming closer. The lights come into view and stop in front of that place where noise and smoke filter into the night air.

A good place to start.

***

Growing up in the 50s and early 60s, in our home, was anything but fun. We lived in constant fear of being physically beaten and emotionally abused by our father. It was during these times I prayed for and wished for a hero to save us.

Yet no hero showed.

No Hopalong, no Superman, no John Wayne. As for prayer, no angel, no Jesus, no God. We were left to fend for ourselves.

It was that time again. Friday evening, and mom loaded my siblings, Rusty, Rossy, Mikey, little Judy and me into the old brown station wagon. Being the oldest at ten, I got to ride shotgun, and my siblings sat in the back. We were all two years apart, the youngest being little Judy at two years old. Rusty and Rossy sat by the windows, with Mikey and little Judy between them. We make our rounds of all the local bars looking for dad. It was payday. We had to find dad before he drank up all his paycheck.

Mom made it a game. The first one to see dad's car got a dipped cone at Pete's Drive-In. Ice cream cones were only five cents and dipped was ten. She made sure we had one after a night of looking for dad.

When we found the bar where dad was drinking, she took me in with her. I think taking me in with her reminded him he had children to provide for. Sometimes my presence prevented dad from hitting her.

Tonight was not one of those nights.

Once in the station wagon, mom turned to us and said, "First, we'll go to the Argon by Pete's Drive-In. If dad isn't there, we will go to the one across the tracks by the skating rink. Okay?" All of us responded enthusiastically, because we knew ice cream awaited us.

None of us knew about skating rinks because we rarely had money for fun things. The skating rink sounded like a fun thing.

Right off the bat we found Dad at the Argon. We could taste the ice cream already.

"Okay, Johnny," mom said. "Let's go in."

Getting out of the car, I followed mom through the door into a noisy, smoke-filled bar. The jukebox played Hank Williams' "Your Cheatin' Heart."

After that night, I hated country music.

We found dad sitting next to a sexy blonde gal. I was too young to understand that was a big no-no, but mom understood immediately, and became visibly angry. Seeing mom angry, I also became angry and took an instant dislike for that gal. Dad and mom got into an argument, lots of hollering and screaming.

Knowing what came next, I moved to the side of the jukebox to be out of the way when the fighting started. A new song played on the jukebox. Johnny Horton sang, "I'm a honky tonk man and I can't seem to stop. I love to give the girls a whirl to the music of an old jukebox…"

Lord, I hate country music.

Slap! Slap! Suddenly, mom's on the floor, her face red with marks. Moving to where she fell, dad picked her up by the neck and slammed her into the concrete wall. Then dad did something I had never seen him do before. He grabbed the telephone cord from the public pay phone, and wrapping it around mom's neck, he pulled tight.

Why is he doing that? I thought. It looks like he's trying to hurt mom. Why don't any of these men stop my dad? I hate them! If only I was strong enough.

Too many beatings taught me I needed to be bigger and stronger to stop dad.

One day I will be.

Someone finally spoke up. "Stop, before you kill her!"

Another person called for an ambulance. Then everybody returned to their drinking, as if nothing happened at all.

That night I hated my dad for the terrible things he did to my mom. He was no longer my dad, but the man who married my mom. It stayed that way until the day he died, forty-four years later.

When the ambulance showed, I went outside to be with my siblings. Walking up to the station wagon, I was met by four faces staring back with wide eyes. They had been staring at the big shiny star atop Pete's Drive-In, where the lights seemed to shoot from the center outward, and high into the night sky. But when the ambulance pulled in front of the Argon, their focus shifted to its flashing bright lights.

Climbing in, I told them what happened and that the ambulance was taking mom to the hospital. Everyone cried, including me. I knew what was on their minds, so I said, "No ice cream tonight."

I would have taken all of us to the hospital to be with mom, but I didn't know where it was. However, I knew where home was just two blocks away.

"We need to go home now," I said. "Rossy and Mikey, hold Rusty's hand. I'll carry little Judy. Let's go."

***

The night creature carefully made his way to the trash bin, behind the building where the ambulance had stopped. He sniffed the air and smelled fear. Sniffing again, he located the source of the fear: the children.

He heard them whimpering as they passed his hiding place.

"Why did dad hurt mom?"

"When will mom come home?"

"Will dad hurt us?"

"What do we do now?"

"Why didn't anyone stop him?"

"If we were bigger we could have stopped him."

Johnny didn't answer their incessant questions. It was all he could do to keep walking. It was the boy the night creature turned his attention to.

Sniffing, he smelled the aroma of woman and man on the boy. The scent of woman was stronger, smelling of anxiety. The man was fear.

The night creature followed.

Within sight of their home, a neighbor's large dog barked and growled at them.

"Run!" Johnny yelled as the dog jumped the fence.

As they ran onto the porch they heard a yelp and then silence. When they reached the safety of their front door, they slammed it shut.

Holding the now lifeless dog in front of him, the night creature whispered, "You should not have tried to harm the children. Now, you're my meal."

Changing course back to the ambulance, he made a detour to the storm drain, dropping off his dinner.

***

From his hiding place not far from the entrance, where he

NIGHT CREATURE

remained unseen, he spotted a woman being carried out of the building and into the vehicle with the flashing lights. Breathing deeply, he smells the aroma that clung to the boy. The vehicle takes off, going wherever it came from.

He waited.

Throughout the evening, the night creature watched people enter and exit the building, but none were of the man the boy feared.

Later that evening, a man stumbled out of the building, clinging to a blonde woman. Sniffing the air, he smelled the scent of fear that had covered the boy.

This was the man.

The night creature stared intently, watching the couple stagger to a car parked behind the building. He silently moved closer.

Opening the passenger door, the woman smiles and climbs in. The man closed the door and the woman promptly passed out.

"Oh great," the man mumbled. "Maybe she'll wake…"

Before he could finish the sentence, the night creature grabbed him by the nape of the neck, lifted him into the air and slammed him onto the roof of the car. Momentarily dazed, he tried to move, but slender claws held him tight. Again, he was lifted and his face slammed into the passenger window.

"Not your woman," his voice growled in his ear.

In the next moment, the man flew through the air twenty feet away, where he rolled to a stop. Staring up in horror, the man spotted a hideous, slinky, slimy and foul smelling creature.

He screamed.

The night creature reached for the man and picked him up. Flinging him another twenty feet, where he landed on the road the children stood earlier. The night creature repeated his torture over and over again, until the man rolled to a stop in front of the home of the children.

Gripping the man by the scruff of his neck, the night creature slammed him onto the porch. "You hurt children or women again, and it will be your last," he growled. "Understand?" The creature bared his fangs and screeched, and the man lost control of his bowls. Peering down at the man in his soiled jeans, the night creature howled with laughter and disappeared into the night.

***

"What's that noise on the porch?" Johnny said, moving to the front window.

Soon five faces peered out the window to investigate the sound. They saw their dad lying on the porch and a hideous creature standing over him.

"Hey!" Rossy cried. "It's the creature from the black lagoon."

Just then, the night creature glanced at the children and grinned. Nodding, the night creature disappeared into the dark. The stunned children closed the curtain, looked at each other and prepared themselves.

***

The man sat up, and shaking his head, cleared the cobwebs.

How did I crap in my pants? he thought. That was a weird nightmare. Must have drunk too much.

He picked himself up and staggered into the house. Once inside, he noticed his children standing in a semi-circle around him.

"What the hell do you think you're going to do?" he shouted.

NIGHT CREATURE

The children stared at him. The older three gripped baseball bats, while Mikey and little Judy held hammers at their sides. Moving in closer, they yelled in unison, "You'll never hurt our mom again."

The man screamed in terror as the baseball bats and hammers swung and connected with flesh and bones.

Thump. Bang. Crunch.

His screams fell on deaf ears.

8. THE LOST GOLD MINE OF IDAHO SPRINGS

By PAUL G BUCKNER

"I gotta tell ya, you've had some crazy ideas before, but a lost gold mine?"

"I know what it sounds like, but it's the real deal," Steve said, talking to his younger brother.

"So, let me get this straight, *Professor X*," Mark said, pausing long enough to recline in his chair and fold his arms behind his head. "Cause I'm a little fuzzy on what it is exactly that you're talking about. A second gold rush, huh?" The three days of coarse beard stubble did little to hide the smirk on his face as he emphasized the word 'professor.' His brown eyes shined with a glint of smugness.

"Very funny. God forbid that I may know something that you don't," Steve replied. "But okay, pull up a chair and shut your trap, mutant. You might actually learn something."

The Turner brothers, both in their early twenties were nearly direct opposites on most subjects. Steve, the oldest was easy-going and relaxed while Mark could be impulsive and at times quite cynical. They discussed the idea of the lost gold mine in the living room of the family farm.

"Yeah, yeah, whatever. Everyone knows about the Gold Rush, you're not telling me anything new, but it was in California in 1849, genius. Duh."

"Actually, forty-eight. January twenty-seventh, 1848 to be precise."

"What?" Mark scoffed, folding his arms.

"The California Gold Rush. It wasn't 1849. It was called that because – oh never mind, that's not important. You get on my last damn nerve."

"Listen, Bub, Joe Montana did *not* play for the San Francisco Forty-*eighters* he didn't play for the San Francisco Fifty…fifty…neers, or whatever. The greatest quarterback in the history of the game played for the forty-niners!" Mark mocked. "And Mom always said you were the smart one. I call bullshit. Mic drop," Mark said, holding his hand out pretending he just dropped a microphone on the floor.

"You're an idiot. You know that, right? You have *got to be* adopted. Now, listen up, ape-ass ugly."

"I've been called worse by better," Mark said, needling his brother again. He grabbed two pecans from a bowl on the nearby coffee table and cracked one open. He cocked his head to one side and stared up at his brother with a raised eyebrow.

Steve sighed and ran a hand through his blond hair in exasperation at his brother's puerility and his own lack of restraint.

"Okay, whatever, but I'm not talking about the California Gold Rush, you moron. I'm talking about the one right here in Colorado, a decade later. The one in California only lasted a few years because most of the gold that was found was what is called placer gold or basically easy pickings. They could pan for it in the creeks and rivers. When it was discovered, the population boomed and when you have most of the gold on top of the ground, and an increase in population, it's not hard to figure why it didn't take long to mine it all. After that, it took specialized equipment to mine for what they call lode gold or veins in the rocks underground. Most people couldn't afford that, thus the ending of the California Gold Rush."

"Okay, great, but I still never heard of the Colorado Gold Rush, and I've lived here all my life," Mark said. "Sure, there are tons of mines all over, and everything is gold this or gold that, but the Colorado Gold Rush? Wasn't it just all one thing, California, Colorado, Utah, all the same thing, right?"

"And once again I must point out the fact that you're an idiot. Now do yourself a favor and shut up and listen."

"Okay, Einstein. Enlighten me."

"In January of 1859, a guy by the name of Jackson discovered a large placer gold deposit near Idaho Springs. Remember placer gold deposits are ones that can be mined by panning? No big deal, but then shortly after, lode gold was found in a few different places not far away. Very big deal, which resulted in another gold rush. Thousands of people made their way up from Kansas and Missouri. Newspapers at the time reported that as many as 100 wagons a day would be seen passing by with emigrants on their way to try their luck at mining."

"Okay, so what does that have to do with that old box of books you found and this conversation?"

"Because in the bottom of that box was this," Steve said, waving his new prized possession in the air like a preacher would a bible on Sunday mornings. "It's a journal. Handwritten by one of those emigrants, Nathaniel Hackett. He and his brother William, along with a cousin named

THE LOST GOLD MINE OF IDAHO SPRINGS

Bradford made their way to the territory seeking their fortune in the gold mines. It's a log of their entire journey. Over a year long. The best part is, it tells about an incredible discovery, a natural cave filled with huge veins of gold. Easy pickings. So much so that they didn't know how they were going to get it all out and keep it a secret."

"I'm sure they figured it out and bled it dry of every last ounce."

"That's just it. I've searched every record that I could get my hands on, and I couldn't find much on these men or a mining claim registered in any of their names."

"So, it's all bogus?"

"No. Far from it. It's real alright. Like I said, I couldn't find much on 'em, but what I did find all match up, the names, the timeline all match up. It's the real deal. The journal's missing several pages, and some of it's faded and illegible, but something happened. It's not clear what, but from what I can gather, the men had mined enough gold by this time that they were going to load their mules and get out with what they could, but that's where the entries stopped." Steve held the journal up for his brother to see. "It picks up again with a final entry, a vow that none of the men would ever go back to the mine again and they would never speak of what they saw, which makes sense given that I couldn't find anything *officially* on the claim."

"Really? What the hell happened that would keep them away from a fortune?" Mark asked, completely taken in by his brother's story.

"That's the million-dollar question isn't it, but the thing is, I think there's enough information in here that could lead us to that lost gold mine."

"Wait a minute," Mark said, putting his feet back on the floor and sitting up, suddenly more interested. "Seriously? You really believe that a hundred and fifty years later, nobody has already found it?"

Steve paced across the living room, giving thought to his brother's argument.

"Have you ever heard of a gold strike anywhere near here? Neither have I. The way the journal describes the discovery, I can see how hundreds or even thousands of people could've walked right by and never seen it. Now, here's where it gets really interesting," Steve said, standing over his brother with a mischievous grin. "I found the journal in that box along with some other stuff. I'm sure that the estate sale folks running the sale had no idea what this was. They just come in and sell everything. Maggie Reese owned the house. Do you remember her?"

"Yeah, everyone knows old-lady Reese. She used to come to every baseball, basketball or football game in town. She wore that old red and white truckers hat with all the pins on it. So? She was a nutjob."

"Eccentric," Steve said pointedly. "Not a nut."

"Potato, tomato, it's all the same."

"No, it really isn't. Nut implies crazy, eccentric implies wealth. She was loaded! Mark, you should've seen the place. It was huge. Who knows how many rooms were in it."

"So, what? A rich nutjob is still a nutjob."

Steve rolled his eyes but continued, "I did a little more digging, and as it turns out, Maggie Reese was married to John Reese which is of no consequence. What's important here is her maiden name. You know, her family name before she was married -"

"You're a regular comedian aren't ya? I know what a damn maiden name is, jackass."

"Good, then you'll be able to add two plus two. Her maiden name was Hackett!"

Mark stood and crossed the room. He turned to meet his brother's eyes.

THE LOST GOLD MINE OF IDAHO SPRINGS

"You mean she was married to one of the gold miners?"

"No, dumbass. She was only eighty-seven when she died last year. Do the math."

Mark punched Steve on the shoulder.

"Ow! You jackass."

"Serves you right!"

"It's not my fault that you're an idiot. Anyway, no, she wasn't the wife, not even a daughter. She is, however, the great-great-granddaughter of Nathaniel Hackett, and what's interesting is, she's never worked a day in her life. No telling how much her estate was worth. The house was huge, but apparently, she also owned hundreds of acres of land and businesses around town."

Mark let out a long, soft whistle. "So, the old-bird was loaded, and they *did* find the gold!"

"I'm betting on it, but according to the journal, they left most of it behind and only got out of the mountains with a handful of pack mules."

"Then, what are we waiting for big brother? Let's go find that gold mine!"

PART II

With her soft, luminous blue eyes and long silky blond hair, Michelle Evers was considered pretty by most standards. This morning, however, she didn't feel pretty. Waking early on the hard surface of the small tent, she was sore and achy from the previous day's hike. She slipped on a fresh pair of socks before sliding into her shoes. Tying her hair up in a bun she stood and stretched to wake her tired muscles. Even in the early morning with no makeup, wearing khaki shorts and a pink tank, she was attractive. Unzipping the tent, she ducked out and made her way to the fire. There were coals from the previous evening's fire still hot. She added a few sticks and built it back up and put on the small pot of coffee before turning back to the tent. Ducking inside she jerked the sleeping bag away from her friend who was softly snoring.

"Rise and shine sleepyhead."

The early morning air was brisk, and the smell of pine mixed with campfire smoke and coffee was a welcome aroma to Jennifer as she stirred in her sleeping bag. She found the early morning cheerfulness of her best friend to be a bit annoying, but the smell of the coffee more than made up for it.

"I'm rising, but I'm not shining," Jenni grumbled, slipping out of the tent and making a beeline for the fire. Grabbing a cup from the downed tree log they used for a seat, she poured it full of the black, steaming liquid.

"How'd you sleep?" Michelle asked.

"Like a rock," she said in a gravely morning voice. "I didn't wake up once all night."

Jennifer scoffed. "I'll say. There was a squirrel or something messing around all night. I got up two or three times to shoo it away and you never even stirred."

"Really? I guess I really must've been tired. It was a long hike yesterday, and that pack isn't light."

"It'll be another long hike today."

"But, not before I get some breakfast," Jennifer said, raising a brow and glancing sideways at her friend. She Brushed back a lock of brown hair out of her face and behind her ears.

Michelle laughed, "It's not like you're going to get bacon and eggs out here. As much as you've complained about the weight of your pack now, I don't think a cast-iron skillet and a pound of bacon would've been a great idea."

"I'd trade the tent for hot, buttery biscuits right now.

These trail mix bars get old fast."

"It's just for a few days. Man-up and grow a pair, would ya?" Michelle teased. "Be right back."

"Where are you going?" Jennifer asked.

"I need to use the ladies room if you must know. My morning urinary continence must not be kept waiting any longer."

"Sorry I asked!"

Jennifer finished her coffee, cleaned the cup, and put it away in her pack. Folding the tent flap back, she ducked inside and pulled on a fresh pair of socks and her hiking shoes before rolling up her sleeping bag. The girls had left home only two days earlier for a three-day weekend hiking trip to the mountains. Both were sophomores in college and avid hikers, never missing a chance to be outdoors. Best friends since grade school, the pair shared many of the same hobbies, and any opportunity to escape to the mountains.

When Jennifer heard the scream, she froze, the sound reverberated through the forest, echoing over the mountain.

***

"That's everything," Mark said, tossing the shovel in the bed of the truck.

"Where the hell is Chris?" Steve said. It was more of a statement than a question.

"Who knows, he said he'd be here by eight. It's almost nine, now! If he thought there was any work to be done, he's going to wait until the very last minute!"

No sooner had Mark finished talking when their attention was drawn to the driveway. An old black Chevy 4X4 came speeding up and slid to a stop in a cloud of dust just a few feet away.

"Glad you ladies didn't leave without me," Chris said, jumping down from the raised off-road vehicle and slamming the door, his small stature a stark contrast to the large truck. He hopped on the running boards, grabbed his gear out of the back and threw it in with the brothers. Decked out in camo from head to toe, complete with boonie hat and silver lensed aviators, he looked rather comical standing in front of the brothers with a big toothy grin. A longtime friend of the brothers, he was never one to be left out. He pulled off the sunglasses, "Hope you got plenty of food."

"Good god man, are you ever on time? Never mind, I think we all know the answer to that, just get in and let's go," Steve said.

"Seriously? That's the thanks I get? You call a fella up in the middle of the night, ask him to drop everything, pack up and be here ready to leave with less than a twenty-four-hour notice, and that's the thanks I get? Contemptable. Purely contemptable!"

The brothers stared back in silence.

"Geez, bust a guy's balls for waking up late why don't ya!"

"If you had been any later, you'd be driving the beast up the mountain by yourself, and I doubt that old jalopy would make it very far. By the way, nice fanny-pack there Peter Pan."

"Jealous much?" Chris snickered.

"Not really, no. It – completes you," Mark laughed.

"Whatever, dude. I'll have you know, within this handy little marsupial pouch is all the essential elements to make life in the wild a little more comfortable," Chris said, unzipping the pack strapped around his waist. "Why you got your toilet paper, wet wipes, pocket knife, fire kit, purifying drinking straw, fishing line complete with hooks and a few assorted lures."

"Enough!" The brothers shouted almost in unison.

"We get it, can we go now, for Pete's sake," Mark said. "Okay, okay. Don't get your panties all wadded up my friend."

"Just move your jalopy of yours out of the driveway and get in, we need to get moving," Steve said.

"Right away, Captain. And take it easy on the ol' girl, she may hear you. The she-beast is old, but she's got a lot of miles left in 'er,"

"Whatever," Steve said sliding behind the wheel. Mark jumped in the passenger side leaving Chris alone in the back seat.

"So, where exactly are we going?" Chris asked. "You were awful mysterious on the phone. Cryptic even."

"I think I have the area pinpointed, within five-mile radius anyway. That's where we'll start our search. The journal is fairly descriptive and using Google Earth I think we should be able to find some of the terrain features. There weren't any mining claims in the entire area. None that I ever found a record of. Stands to reason that the mine has stayed hidden all this time," Steve said.

"So, old lady Reese is the great-granddaughter of this miner huh?"

"Yeah, and I've done some digging on her too. For someone to be so crazy wealthy and never have worked a day, tells me that's old money. I'm sure that they found that mine, but unlike others, they didn't get gold fever. Basically, they hit the jackpot and cashed out. Pretty smart if you ask me."

"I wonder why? I mean, why not stake a claim and work the mine. If it were that rich, it would only make sense that they would be like everyone else and work it 'til it's dry."

"I wondered that too, but according to a few passages that I could make out in the journal, something happened. Whatever it was, scared them off. I can't imagine what that might have been. These were tough, rugged frontiersmen that battled more than the elements in their day."

Mark asked, "Do you think it could've been Indians? There had to be Native American tribes around, don't you think? Encroachment is more than enough cause to run 'em off, I'd think."

"No idea," Steve said. "All I could gather is they were attacked several times when they were working the mine. Their supplies were running low, and they had lots of gold to get out, so they packed up what they could on the mules and hightailed it out of there. It could've been marauders, Indians, or even bears."

"So, what's the plan?" Chris asked.

"We find it!" Mark said.

"Duh! I kinda figured that, smartass."

Steve laughed. "There's an old logging road we need to find just off the highway. We'll take it as far as we can, and then we'll have to hoof it. I think it'll take us a couple of days depending on how far that road goes back. Then, we do a grid search for signs of the cave. The good thing is, ol' Hackett was pretty descriptive. I'm sure we can find it."

They drove for the better part of the day before Steve found the turnoff that led to the campground. Just as he turned off the highway and rounded a curve, he slammed on the brakes.

Mark saw the obstruction too but had been riding along in silence mesmerized by the thrumming of the wheels on the road, he was slow to react. His seat-belt restrained him from the sudden stop, but not without its consequences.

"What the hell, man? That frikkin hurt!" Mark said,

rubbing his shoulder.

"Sorry," Steve said, trying not to laugh.

Chris, who had been asleep in the back seat was not as lucky. He wasn't wearing a seat-belt and was launched into the back of the front seats and swiftly deposited into the floorboard.

The Gaines brothers felt the impact and turned to look but couldn't see him.

"You okay back there?"

Two seconds later a long skinny arm shot up. Waving like a flag of surrender, Chris gave a thumbs up. "I'm okay," he squeaked.

Steve shifted into park, turned the ignition key off and got out to inspect the iron-post gate that stretched across the road.

"Now what?" Mark asked.

"I didn't come all this way to turn back because of a closed road," Steve said grinning. He walked over to the end of the gate and began moving some branches and rocks. "I think we can get around it. There's not a fence."

"Great, not only do I get body-slammed on this trip, probably have broken ribs and fractured vertebrae, but I also get to spend jail time for trespassing with brothers Grimm!" Chris complained.

"Do you ever quit your whining, ya big baby? Mark said. "There's not a *no trespassing*' sign hanging on the gate. Probably just an old logging road that the state didn't want to maintain. It's still public land."

"Let's check it out," Steve said climbing back in the truck.

There was just enough room to get the gray Z71 past the gate. They cleared and gate and bounced along the abandoned road. Several areas had been all but washed out, but the four-wheel drive had little issue navigating the rough, dry terrain.

"How far do you think it goes?" Chris asked.

"Not sure exactly, but we'll go as far as we can and take a look at the GPS. No matter what, we're going to be doing a lot of hiking."

"Why didn't you go around on highway twelve and go up to Port Falls Camp Ground?"

"Well, let's see numbnuts. If we go into a public campground with RV's and blue-hairs everywhere you turn, it might be a little suspicious to see three guys carrying a metal detector and shovels into the woods."

"I get your point."

Branches slapped at the truck as they pushed past them. They were running out of road!

"I think we better find a good place to stop and make camp. Doesn't look like this old road's going much further," Mark said

"Looks like the GPS shows us only a few clicks from where I dropped the pin on the map. I was hoping to get a lot closer than that."

"I think the problem is the road's been pretty level and just curving around. It doesn't go *up* the mountain," Mark emphasized. "Not nearly as much as it should. Are you sure it's the right one?"

"Yeah, it's the right one, but it's not been used in years."

"Then that means we'll be hiking a lot more *up* than anything," Mark groaned.

Chris leaned forward pointing at the road ahead, "I hope you brought a chainsaw. That's one big ass dead tree across the road."

Steve stopped the truck just in front of the downed Birch that covered the entire road. The forest growth was too thick in the area to go around so, he turned off the ignition and jumped out.

THE LOST GOLD MINE OF IDAHO SPRINGS

"Nothing else to do but start cutting branches, fellas. I have a limb saw in my pack."

"I've got a hatchet here somewhere," Mark said.

Chris threw open the door and stood on the side step, "How much further up the road is it? Maybe we can find a place to camp right here?"

"Not a chance big man," Mark said as he came around to their side of the truck. "It's at least four or five more miles back in there. I'm not packing all this crap any further than what I have to."

***

An hour later, Steve parked the truck in a small grove of Gambel Oaks and climbed out.

"I didn't think it would take this long to get here," Mark said as he slammed the door getting out.

"It shouldn't have," Steve said. "But when you stop every thirty minutes for a pee break, not to mention the two-hour lunch at the truck stop, closed gates, chopping down trees to get through on this damn road, I think we're lucky to get here before dark."

After the men had cut the tree up enough to get the truck through, Chris jumped in the back seat and lay down. He was asleep within minutes. The slamming door woke him.

"What the hell?" Chris said. It took a moment for clarity to sink in. Once he had his bearings, he opened the door and jumped out.

"Glad you could join us sleeping beauty," Mark laughed. "We already found the gold and ready to head back now."

Chris yawned loudly and stepped around behind the truck. "*Riiiight.* Cutting up that tree wore me out. Pardon me while I water the petunias."

"Let's get the tent set up and find some firewood before it gets dark on us. The sun sits fast up here in the mountains," Steve suggested.

Mark used a hatchet to cut up dead tree branches and had a fire going in no time. Once the tent was set up, and sleeping bags unrolled they settled near the fire to discuss their plans.

Chris poked at the flames with a long stick. "Man, this is the life fellas. I could live like this forever."

"You say that now, but we'll see if you still feel that way after a two-day hike up this mountain," Steve laughed.

"Not talking about climbing a mountain with the Bert and Ernie," Chris sighed deeply, "I just meant this part, you know, sitting beside a warm fire deep in the woods with no cell phones, no boss yelling at me, no idiot drivers honking their horns and cutting me off."

"Yeah, I know what you mean. It's peaceful up here, that's for sure," Steve said. "Speaking of no cell phone coverage, I picked up a map of the area. We gotta go in pure analog. Sort of, I mean I doubt we will get any reception up here at all, but we have the Garmin."

"Good thinking, but did you happen to bring a compass just in case?" Mark asked.

"Well, yeah. I'm not an idiot."

"That's open for debate."

Steve was too tired to bicker with his younger brother. He let the comment slide. "We need to get an early start and use all the daylight we can."

"So, what *is* the plan for tomorrow?" Chris asked while checking the magazine in the .45 he had brought with him for protection.

"Sweet! That new?" Mark asked.

"Yeah, got it last week. Never can be too careful up here," Chris said. He dropped the mag and pulled the slide

THE LOST GOLD MINE OF IDAHO SPRINGS

back to reveal an empty chamber before handing it to Mark to inspect.

Steve ignored their side conversation, "We'll follow the ridge for five miles or so before we leave it and make our way south. It shouldn't take long to reach that point, maybe four or five hours, but once we leave the trail, I suspect the terrain to get much tougher and slow us down considerably."

"That doesn't seem far away from lots of people," Chris commented.

"Yeah, really!" Mark said. "I mean, this entire area has been logged, decades ago sure, but still that means that lots of people have been all over this mountain. Surely, someone's found the mine by now. How could it have stayed hidden all this time.?"

Steve laughed, "Oh, no. Once we leave the trail, it'll take us the rest of the day, maybe longer, to get to the area where we really start our search. Well away from any public hiking areas. I've checked the map several times. I'm hoping that the route will keep us near fresh water along the way. With all the snow melt still coming down, that shouldn't be a problem."

The men talked quietly by the fire a bit more before turning in for the evening. Chris, having napped most of the drive up, decided to sit up awhile and enjoy the peace and quiet of the late evening.

"Goodnight fellas, I'll be in soon. I'll make sure to have enough wood on the fire to keep it going all night." He tossed a few more pieces of wood on the fire then leaned back against a large log someone had dragged near to use as a seat. It was a quiet and peaceful evening as he watched the flames dance in the darkness.

He didn't know how long he had slept or what woke him up, but he was wide awake now, and all his senses on high alert, the hair on the back of his neck tingled. The fire had died down to nothing more than a soft glow of embers. He kept still and quiet, listening for any noise out of the ordinary. There it was again. A soft rustling in the woods not far behind where he sat as if whatever it was, was trying to sneak up on the camp. More noticeably, whoever it was, walked on two feet. Chris was hidden behind the log, and with no fire behind him, he knew there would be no silhouette for him to be spotted. His hand slowly reached for the .45 he kept on his hip. The rustling stopped. Judging from the sound, whoever, or whatever was in the woods creeping up on him, wasn't more than twenty feet away. *Where is my flashlight*, he thought? He saw it lying just a few feet away. He grabbed it with his left hand while holding his pistol in his right. Rolling onto his knees, he aimed the gun and flashlight straight at the direction of the noise.

"Whoever you are, you better show yourself before I start spraying lead," he shouted.

He strained to hear any movements. Nothing.

"I mean it. You better come on out," His voice breaking.

He heard a sudden crashing in the underbrush just to the left of his light. He adjusted his aim and waited. He was nervous, but not scared as long as he had his pistol for protection.

The tent flap suddenly zipped open, and someone stumbled out.

It was Mark.

"What's going on?" Mark asked.

"There's someone out there trying to sneak up on us."

"Seriously, dude, you need to chill with the Rambo shit. You're gonna get someone killed."

THE LOST GOLD MINE OF IDAHO SPRINGS

"Yeah, like me! You idiot!" Steve shouted from the woods. He stepped out from the trail and walked back toward the fire. "Get that damn light out of my eyes, you're blinding me. Dear lord, I had to go take a leak and couldn't find my flashlight."

"Sorry dude, my bad," Chris said, relaxing. "But how was I supposed to know that?"

"Because I walked right by you on my way out, you moron. Jeez, dude, you've been watching too much TV."

"I'm going back to bed," Mark said, ducking inside the tent.

"Yeah, I guess I will too," Chris muttered, following the brothers.

***

Jennifer heard the scream and didn't hesitate. The girls never hiked without some sort of protection. She rifled through her pack until she found what she was looking for. Darting from the tent, she ran as fast as she could maneuver through the brush toward the sound of Michelle's voice.

"Chelle," Jennifer shouted. "I'm coming?" She saw a flash of movement and changed directions to meet her friend in a small clearing.

"There's something out there," she panted. "Not sure what it was, but, I don't know, a bear maybe. A person, I don't know. Let's just get out of here."

"Where was it? How far away?"

"I don't know. Let's just go."

"Okay, calm down and take a deep breath. In through your nose and out your mouth. Slow your heart rate down, or you're gonna keel over."

"You don't understand. Let's go."

When they got back to the camp, Michelle explained. "I was doing my business when I saw it. I just took off running. Maybe it was a bear, I don't know, but there shouldn't be anyone out here. I'm sure I scared it more than it scared me."

Jennifer laughed. "I'm sure you did. I'm going to have a quick look around."

"No, don't go out there. Let's just get packed up and leave the area."

"It's okay, I have the Trail Guard with me," Jennifer said, holding the can of bear spray up. "I'm just going to have a quick look around to make sure it's not following us. I won't go far, just start packing up. I'll be right back."

Jennifer made her way up the trail, stopping several times to look around and listen for anything out of the ordinary. When she reached the large pinion tree that Michelle had described to her, she studied the ground all around it but found nothing. She turned to start back when she heard something rustling in the bushes not far away. She looked around to make sure she had an escape route plan and holding the can up, she stood her ground and waited. A moment later, the brush parted revealing the source. She didn't bother with the spray. She ran as fast as she could back to the camp.

"Pack it up, let's get out of here."

"What was it? What did you see? Is it chasing you? Is it a bear?" Michelle asked anxiously.

Jennifer grabbed Michelle's shoulder and bent over to catch her breath before talking.

"No, not a bear. It was a huge, black and white skunk!"

"Seriously? Are you kidding? That's *not* what I saw, I swear!"

"I don't know and right now don't care. Let's get going."

"Sounds good to me," Michelle said.

Twenty minutes later the girls departed camp.
"We should probably go around, just in case your cute little friend is still out there," Jennifer said.
"Probably not a bad idea. We can skirt around through the woods and meet back up with the trail later. I just don't want whoever, or *what*ever that was to follow us."

PART III

Steve was the first one up that morning. Not that the sun found him asleep. He lay awake most of the night reading through the journal, thinking about what it must have been like for those miners. One passage stood out.

> *Bears? We are not sure. But we are fearful with each passing night. If we are to make it home, we are in need of packing out as much of our fortune that the remaining mules can carry. We have made a pact, if we get out of this God-forbidden country, we shall never return – Nat. H*

"Tell me again why I have to be the one to carry all this shit?" Chris asked.
Steve hefted the backpack to Chris's shoulders and helped him get it adjusted. "Because I have to carry the Garmin and navigate. I may need to scout ahead and stuff. Besides, you're a badass. Remember?"
"I'm also the smallest guy here!"
"Don't know why you're all pissed off," Mark said. "I'm

the one carrying this stupid metal detector, and the tent, not to mention most of the food."

"If you two ladies are done bitching, think we can get started?" Steve said, "Chris put this topo map in your cute little fanny pack, so we have quick access."

Steve turned and led the way on a game trail that seemed to point in the general direction they were headed.

Mark turned to follow his brother just as Chris stepped onto a large rock and jumped on the trail. Their backpacks collided mid-stride.

"Hey, watch where you're going, Magellan!" Mark said, giving Chris a playful shove that sent him stumbling to the side of the trail.

"Jackass! I was moving way before your pachyderm carcass lumbered out in front of me. It's a good thing my ninja reflexes kicked in."

Steve groaned and rolled his eyes but didn't stop to watch the two. They were following him now. The intrepid explorers had a long way to go over rough terrain, and he planned on taking advantage of all the daylight they could get.

The woods, though a misty gray in the early morning hours, were easily navigable. Steve kept to a game trail discovered as they began the first leg of their trek. He kept the Garmin and gave the map to Chris to keep in his fanny pack for quick reference. Their goal for the first half of the day was just to get to the top of the ridge cap. They hoped to do so by noon. There, they would take a short break then follow the ridge north. Steve had researched the area before their trip and used satellite images to pinpoint exact coordinates and distances between each one as he had them marked on the map.

Chris stepped on a dead tree branch snapping it under the weight of his boots with a resounding crack. The action caused a Raven perched on a tree some distance away to caw loudly and flap off. Steve shot a glance over at him.

"Sorry," Chris shrugged before continuing. A few minutes later he spoke up again. "Though I'm not sure why. I mean, we've been walking all quiet-like, like we're trying to sneak out of the church in the middle of the sermon to go have a cigarette or something."

"Yeah, I guess we have at that," Steve said. "Not sure why either." He chuckled a bit. "I guess it's just so quiet in here, tends to force that behavior through the power of suggestion. Really no reason for us to worry about disturbing anyone," Steve laughed.

Mark brushed past a long branch that caught on his pack. The limb snapped back slapping Chris on the check.

"Ow!" Chris shouted. "WTF dude?"

Mark laughed, "Sorry about that. What happened to your ninja reflexes?"

"You're gonna think ninja. That freakin' hurt ya mangy cur!"

"Sorry man, I'll try to be more careful," Mark smirked. He was never surprised by Chris's actions, or words. They had known each other before they could even remember and were more like family than merely friends. This was just the way they carried on.

Steve had prodded along ahead of the two but had now stopped in a small clearing to look at the GPS and the map.

"What gives big brother?" Mark asked.

"Well," Steve began then suddenly paused a moment before continuing. "We've been following this game trail for a few hours but, unfortunately, seems to turn here and head back down the mountain. We're gonna have to leave it and turn up. It'll probably get a little hairier from here on out." He turned and walked off quickly not waiting for debate from the others.

"I'm right behind you. Mark can ride drag," Chris quipped as he hurriedly jumped in behind Steve cutting Mark off with a raised brow and a glib look.

"Whatever," Mark said, rolling his eyes.

***

Michelle stood on a rocky outcropping overlooking a small valley below. The wind, blowing from the south, tossed about several locks of her long blond hair that had escaped the tight bun on her head, and her face was dirty from with sweat and dirt of countless hours fighting the elements of the mountain, a feeling she loved. Pine trees that once stood tall and proud now lay scattered in clumps at the bottom of the steep slope, uprooted from years of erosion and what appeared to be a recent washout. A small game trail wound down the steep hill just beneath her which may be safe enough for small animals but could prove to be too much of an obstacle for the hikers. From her position, she could also see the peaks and valleys of several other mountain tops far off in the distance. Though, a beautiful panorama, one far too dangerous for the moment.

"Precarious at best," Michelle mumbled.

"What was that?" Jennifer asked.

Michelle turned and smiled at her friend. "The slope. It looks too dangerous. I'd rather go around. It'll take a little longer, but it'll be safer."

"So much for a shortcut," Jennifer laughed. "Besides, we came for the scenery, right?"

Michelle laughed along with her friend. "Yeah, true. Besides, how were we to know the trail was washed out?"

"It wasn't recent, though."

"No, you're right, happened some time ago, but we've not been here in a few years now."

Jennifer thought about it as she watched a monarch butterfly flitting off among the weeds and wildflowers. "Yeah, at least two years since we hiked it last."

"I would like to get back to the main trail before it gets dark so that we can set up camp for the night. With any luck, it won't rain anymore today," Michelle said.

"I'm not so sure about that. I mean, look at the sky. Could break lose any minute and being that we have to go around this washout, it may take hours. It's already after two. I don't want to go back though, think we just circle around and pick up the main trail on the other side?"

"I don't see why not. I don't want to back-track either."

"Well then, let's get moving.

The girls turned away from the rocky ledge, leaped over the scattered rocks left uprooted from the tree roots when the giant sentries lost their perch on the rim and landed with ease back on the dirt path. As Jennifer fell in step behind Michelle, an unkindness of ravens in the woods far below flocked away. Their wings beating hard against the wind, their shrill cries floating eerily on the breeze and echoing through the canyon.

***

"Shouldn't we have reached the top of the ridge by now?" Chris asked.

"It's not much further – maybe another hour," Steve answered. His face flush from physical exertion.

"I hope to God it is," Mark said. "I'm starving, not to mention tired as hell carrying all this crap."

"I gotta take a leak. You guys keep going. I'll catch up in a few," Chris said.

"Dude, you just did not more than half an hour ago. You have the bladder the size of an acorn, I swear."

Chris shot Mark a dirty look as he unzipped his camouflage pants. "That's because my body has to make room for *this* monster."

"Oh, dear lord," Mark said with disgust and turning away to follow Steve. "Just catch up when you're done playing with yourself."

Chris watched the brothers leave then slid behind a large tree. He wasn't worried about getting too far behind, he was no stranger to the woods and having tracked plenty of deer during hunting season, following the trail of two men slogging their way through dense forests and vegetation would be simple.

He was small in stature, but Chris Brady made up for it with blustery bravado. He was a good-natured and a fun guy to be around. He grew up near the Turner brothers and had been best friends with them since any of the boys could remember. Now in their early twenties, they couldn't spend as much time together doing the things they used to like hunting, fishing, and camping so, this trip was a welcome adventure. Steve had gone off to college right after high school, Mark went to a welding school, bought his own rig and traveled the country from job site to job site. Chris was the only one that stayed in Idaho Springs after graduating. He had worked in the local pizza restaurant through high school and now managed it. He never had the desire to continue to college. He was happy and content with staying home.

He dropped his backpack and laid it nearby. It felt good to be relieved of the heavy burden even if for only a short time. The pack weighed nearly sixty pounds, and for Chris, that meant over thirty-five percent of his own body weight which was more than most amateur hikers would dare to carry. He shook his arms and legs out to loosen up and rotated his shoulders several times while walking around the area. Satisfied the others were far enough away, he took off his fanny pack, unzipped it and removed the few items he needed. Finding a branch just above his head, he hung the pack over it before unstrapping his pistol and pitching it on top of the backpack. He was tired and sore even though the group hadn't traveled far yet.

***

"Finally," Steve said. "I thought we'd never get to this ridge."

"You're telling me, I'm exhausted," Mark said. "Looks like a good place to wait for Chris to catch up too. Lots of rocks along this ridge and as good a tracker as he is, even he may have trouble following our trail over this terrain."

"Yeah, good idea and it's a lot later in the day than I had anticipated, but look over there, fresh water to fill the water packs," Steve said indicating a runoff of crystal clear snowmelt. He dropped his backpack and knelt beside the small stream. Cupping his hands, he drank deeply. "Ah, that's good stuff."

"I'll fill 'em in a minute. I gotta get this pack off and sit down before I collapse," Mark said.

Mark found a cool spot out of the wind on the shady side of a large boulder and dropped to the ground. He leaned against the rock and blew out a breath of air, relaxing for the moment. Even though the temperature wasn't necessarily hot, the physical exertion and arid climate was taking its toll on him. He hadn't hiked this much in over a year, and he was feeling it. His legs were aching, but the cool earth beneath him felt good enough to take his mind off it for the moment.

"I figured Chris would've caught up by now," Steve commented.

"Yeah, I know. I would guess that it was about a half a click back where we left him. Surely, he'll be along any minute."

Steve turned suddenly, "What was that?"

"What was what?" Mark asked, sitting up.

"I heard something. Sounded like a growl. Shhh," Steve said, cocking his head and straining to hear.

Mark slowly rose to his feet as quietly as he could. He backed away from the rocks and stopped when he was next to his brother. A slow, scraping sound came from the other side of the boulders accompanied by a low-pitched growl. He whispered, "I heard it too, mountain lion?" he asked.

"Not sure," Steve said, looking around for a weapon.

Suddenly a shadow flashed accompanied by a loud piercing scream coming from the rocks above them. The brothers stood shoulder to shoulder to meet the attack head-on. The shadow leaped in front of them from the top of the boulder and landed with a heavy thud just in front of them rolling and then collapsing in a heap.

Chris lay on his back at the feet of the brothers, rolling back and forth clutching his knee to his chest and moaning.

Mark took the opportunity to kick him.

"Ow! WTF dude?" Chris whimpered. "Have you no sympathy for a dying man?" He laughed.

"You're lucky I didn't kick you square in the junk, you jackass."

"Ha! Chris was laughing hysterically now, "You should've seen the looks on your faces. Oh wow, classic, epic even."

Steve turned away and walked back over to the water stream and began filling his water bladder.

"You're an imbecile."

"That may be true Stevie T, but I'm a damned funny one."

Mark scoffed. "Only in your head. Personally, I think you're just an idiot. Not the idiot savant type, but the idiot can't tie your own shoelaces type, can't walk and chew gum at the same time type, or even…"

"I get it, dude. Jeez. Go busting a guy's balls why don't ya," Chris said.

Mark joined his brother at the stream and filled his water bladders with the fresh and cold water of the Rockies after drinking deeply.

"Steve, it's getting kinda late, we should probably get moving now that the moron's back, don't ya think?

Steve glanced over at Chris who was limping around and mumbling about his knee.

"Yeah, grab your gear and let's get moving. Chris, get your stuff, let's go."

"Jeez fellas, can't a guy get a little break first? You've been sacked up right here under the shade for a good twenty minutes," Chris said walking around the giant boulder to retrieve his backpack before he tried to scare his friends.

"Yeah, I suppose it'll give me a chance to look over the topography again, make sure we're on the right track. You got the map."

"Yeah, I got it right -" Chris began but stopped short when he realized he didn't have his fanny pack. His eyes widened when he remembered that he forgot to get off the tree he had hung it on in the woods when he had stopped earlier. "Uhm, I'd really like to, but I don't have it."

"How could you have lost it?" Mark asked.

"It's not lost. I know exactly where it is."

"Oh, dear lord," Steve said. "Where is it?"

"Hanging in a tree where I just came from."

"Damn! I guess we don't necessarily need the map." Steve said.

"Yeah, but I have important stuff in that pack, not to mention a small derringer."

"Are you kidding me? How many guns do you need?" Mark said.

Steve threw his hands up in disgust, "You're killing me, Smalls! Are we ever going to actually look for the gold mine?"

"The good news is, I know exactly where I left it. The bad news is, we'll lose another hour of daylight. It's hanging from a tree where I stopped to use the bathroom."

"Then I suggest you hot-foot it back to that tree and retrieve it. We'll have to set up camp here tonight. Was hoping to make it a lot further than this before we stopped, but, nothing else to do."

"Sorry fellas, don't suppose either of you want to tag along?"

They both stared at him as if they couldn't believe he would even ask such as ridiculous question.

"We'll get camp set up while you're gone," Steve said turning away.

"Well, alrighty then. I see how I rate. I'll be back in a bit," Chris said. He turned and trotted back down the trail.

***

Though some areas were dark and impenetrable by most sunlight due to the canopy of the massive old tree growth, Chris had no trouble finding his way back down the trail. In his haste to catch up to his buddies earlier, he had forgotten that he had hung his fanny pack containing the map among other things on a tree branch.

Half an hour later he arrived. He knew he had the right place because his pack was now laying on the ground, open and all the contents had been scattered about.

"What the hell!"

His first reaction was disbelief. His second, was worry.

PART IIIV

"I'll get the tent set up if you want to gather up some wood for a fire tonight?" Steve suggested.

"Sure thing, I've got the water bottles filled," Mark replied.

Steve unrolled the tent and began setting it up on a level area he had brushed off with a tree branch. As he leaned down to hammer in a stake, a drop of sweat formed on his temple. It would drop into his eye at any moment, but his hands were full with the hammer and the guy-line for the tent. He tossed his head back and tried his best to use his shoulder to wipe it away, but it was too late. The small droplet dribbled down into his right eye.

"Ah, man!" He exclaimed dropping his hammer and the line.

"What's wrong with you?" Mark asked.

"Sweat and hair in my eye."

Mark shrugged his shoulders and continued gathering small dead limbs for a fire.

Steve stood and walked over to the stream. Kneeling next to the edge he reached in and splashed some on his face before dipping his head into the cold running water. It wasn't hot, but the physical exertion made it feel much warmer than it was. He also tended to sweat a lot.

Before he had gone to college, he was very active and spent a great deal of time outdoors. Steve loved to snowboard during the winter, but he preferred summer activities like swimming and hiking. In high school, he played sports, but he was more prone to academics.

"Remind me I need a haircut when we get home," Steve said. "This stuff is getting too long. I'm starting to feel like a sheepdog."

His brother laughed. "You're starting to look like one too."

Steve ran his hands over his wet hair and smoothed it back out of his face. The cold water felt refreshing.

"You say that, but you could definitely use one too ya know. That mess on your head looks like a rooster exploded," Steve said laughing.

"Yeah, but I'm not complaining about mine."

"If you could see that mop now right now, you might change your tune," Steve said.

"Don't be a hater. You know how the ladies swoon over these locks. I have my choice. It's kinda like I'm Samson or something," Mark joked.

"Please, I saw the last one you dated. I thought you'd lost a bet!"

Mark stood and stared at his brother in silent indignation.

"What? No witty come-back little brother?" Steve taunted.

"There's really no need to further the humiliation that I could bestow upon you. I've not seen your ugly ass date any *thing*, let alone any – *one*!" Mark said haughtily.

"That's only because I'm a little pickier than you. I swear, your only caveat to dating is that they can walk and breath unassisted. Critical thinking skills need not apply."

"Don't forget good looking. Besides, the only critical thinking skills they need to have is the ability to bait a hook, run a trot-line or shoot a deer. Other than that, just look good."

Steve, tired of the banter, shrugged it off and went back to work on the tent. Once he had the tie-downs secure, he unrolled his sleeping bag and tossed it on the floor.

"Think I'll take a short nap."

***

When Chris found the brothers exploring the campsite shortly after his return and explained how he had found his belongings.

"I'm telling you guys, no squirrel could've done that," he explained. "It was unzipped! That means opposable thumbs. I've never seen a squirrel with opposable thumbs."

"Could've been aliens. You should probably check to make sure they didn't probe you and then wipe your memory. You *are* walking a little bow-legged?" Mark joked.

"Very funny ya jerk. Seriously, when I got back, everything was taken out of the pack and just dumped out on the ground. No way could an animal have unzipped it."

Steve, who was sitting on a rock near the tent agreed with Chris.

"I think you're right about that."

"Thank you!" Chris said as he shot a glare at Mark. "I'm glad to see that one of you Turner brothers has a little common sense about 'em."

"I said I agreed with you that it couldn't have been an animal that unzipped it, but I do believe that an animal pilfered it because you left it unzipped when you hung it up in the tree. A bird could've seen it and took any paper to build a nest with. That map is probably in some Crow's nest as we speak. Way to go, Chris."

"There, that's a buyable explanation," Mark chimed in.

"I know for a fact that I zipped it back. I know I did. You can't convince me otherwise. I was there, I did it. It wasn't more than a few hours ago. I think I'd remember."

"Whatever dude," Mark said. "Just man up and fess up

that you lost the map."

"I didn't just lose the map. I mean, yeah, I lost it, but not my fault. Besides, if it was a person, I don't think they would have left it behind especially my derringer. They would've taken it with 'em. It had to be an animal that scattered it all out. As for a bird taking the map, yeah maybe, but why not all the toilet paper they had unraveled. That would've been easier for 'em to carry off."

"I think you answered your own question. It was all unraveled so, birds may have done that, but it was too long to carry off. The map being folded up was small and lightweight, easy pickings." Steve sighed. "At least we still have the Garmin, the map was just for backup."

"Yeah, well – anyway, what's for supper?" Chris asked.

"The same thing that we had for breakfast and the same thing we had for lunch, and the same thing that we had the day before," Steve laughed, pulling out an energy bar and tossing it to him.

"Oh boy, can't wait."

"There's always twigs and berries," Steve said. "Being the outdoorsman that you are, why don't we have steaks on the fire?"

"Too heavy, I'd rather have some fresh trout," Mark said. "Why don't you catch us some fish?"

"Oh, and how do you expect me to do that? Stick my head in the water and bite one with my teeth? Besides, I doubt there's any fish in this stream. Probably just snow melt."

"That doesn't mean there's not any fish in it. Besides, I just got a whiff of something from upwind that smells an awful lot like dead fish. Whew, nasty," Steve said wrinkling his nose.

"OMG dude, are you sure that's fish? I just caught the smell of it too. That's one-hundred percent, grade-A stamped guaranteed frikkin' nasty. Putrid! Smells like rotting carcass," Mark said.

"Great place for a campsite. You two win the hiker of the year award for campsite location. Downwind of a stagnate pool of Dances with Wolves pond carcasses. I can't leave ya'll alone for one minute."

"Oh please, that's not any worse than your feet. Which by the way, I'll need you to wash those things, or you are NOT sleeping in the tent tonight."

"I don't mind sleeping outside and away from your snoring. You sound like a cave full of hibernating bears for God's sake."

Steve stood and looked toward the sky, "The wind is changing directions again, so maybe we can stay downwind of whatever that smell is," he said as he turned back to the others. "It feels a colder too, rain maybe."

Mark gave Chris a smug grin, "You're still sleeping outside."

***

Though the evening was blustery, it was not unpleasant. The wind drifted through the forest, carrying the sharp scent of junipers mixed with the sweet, pungent smell of firewood smoke. Michelle sat next to the campfire reading her Kindle while Jenni, sitting across from her, fidgeted with a couple of fruit bars in her hands.

"This is nice, don't you think? Don't get me wrong or anything, I do miss my TV, my hair-dryer, curling iron, makeup, clean bathroom," Jennifer said, breaking the silence.

"You're bored, aren't you?"

"Yup, I sure am. Was thinking I was hungry, but neither one of these things look appealing to me. Dry leaves and mud almost seem better." Jenni laughed. Her laughter was contagious, and soon Michelle found herself joining in.

"Buck up, you'll be back to your creature comforts of home in a few days. Right now, just try enjoying the break away from all the other," Michelle hesitated a moment before continuing, "Junk – that goes along with it."

"Such as?"

"Such as getting up at 7 a.m. and going to class, cramming for finals, having Dr. Haiden stare at your boobs during his lectures, shall I go on?"

"No, you had me at Dr. Haiden staring at my boobs. Eh! Just think, I'll have to have one more class with him next semester. The guy makes my skin crawl. Does he really think any girl would be dumb enough to sleep with him for a grade?"

"I know right," Michelle laughed.

"You're right though, breaking away for a few days was a great idea. I can feel the stress drain away,"

Michelle closed her Kindle. "I think I'll turn in."

"Yeah, probably not a bad -"

Lightning suddenly splintered across the sky accompanied by booming thunder as if it were an orchestra solo of tympani drums rumbling over the mountain. Shards of pure white energy strobed against a black backdrop and crackled in a dozen directions illuminating the mountain in an eerie effect.

"Oh shit!" Michelle said. "That scared the hell out of me."

"Maybe we should stake the tent down extra tight tonight," Jenni said as she watched mother nature's fireworks show.

"Agreed. I didn't bring any rain gear. Didn't think I'd need it."

"Me either," Jenni said. Her amber eyes reflected the

firelight and her brows wrinkled in worry as she looked at her friend.

"Probably just a little summer thing and it'll blow itself out long before any rain comes from it," Michelle said softly, unable to hide the worry in her voice.

***

The rain pelted the men's tent trying to penetrate the soft fabric with each wind-driven spike, but the men had taken caution to drive the stakes deep and pull the lines tight. Updrafts pushed and tugged against dome as if trying to uproot it and send it and all occupants flying off the mountain. The tent had seen more than a handful or thunderstorms, and the mesh had tightened through the use enough, so the men felt comfortable enough not to get drenched. The sleeping bags were lightweight and kept the cold night air at bay.

Chris lay on his mat with his hands cradling his head, staring up at the top of the tent watching the bursts of lightning expose the rippling of the fabric.

"I think we'll be fine as long as it doesn't last all night," Steve said.

"Yeah, sometimes these things come in like a lion and leave like a lamb in minutes," Mark said in the cover of darkness.

"It must be forty degrees. I'm freezing," Steve said as he pulled on a fresh pair of socks and a long-sleeved t-shirt. "Sure wished we had a fire going in here."

Mark laughed, "We could build one, but Chris may not appreciate us using his sleeping bag and clothes for it."

Chris harrumphed, "And you thought I was nuts for packing my long johns. I'm quite toasty over here."

"Make no mistake there, probe-boy, we don't think

you're nuts for that, we just think you're nuts in general."

"You're a real jerk, do you know that?"

"I've been told that on more than a few occasions."

"But, since you bring it up," Chris began. "I've been thinking about that. I know for a fact that I zipped that bag back up when I hung it on the limb. Otherwise, everything would've fallen out. I just don't see who or what could've unzipped it and dumped everything out like that."

"Just too bad you lost the map," Mark replied.

"Just too bad you're a moron," Chris said throwing one of his dirty socks in Mark's direction.

Steve rolled over and pulled his sleeping bag up over his head.

"If you two are going to talk all night, try to keep it down to a dull roar, maybe a few less decibels than the storm. I'm gonna try to get some sleep."

"I have no idea how you could possibly sleep through this storm, dude. It feels like it's going to blow this tent along with all three of us into the next county," Chris said.

"It's easy, just roll over and close my eyes."

PART V

Michelle hammered at the tent stake with a rock trying desperately to get it to hold. The wind raged against the small red and blue tent illuminated through the torrential downpour by constant streaks of bolt lightning. Jennifer did her best to keep the guy-line taught but struggled for a firm hand-hold.

"Almost got it!" Michelle shouted above the enraged roar of the storm.

The wind had pulled the stake loose during the night which allowed the wind to push under the tent. The two women scrambled out of their bedrolls as quickly as they could to get it secured. The rain was cold in the mountains, and they were ill-equipped for it. Michelle's hands were freezing. The rock she was using as a hammer suddenly slipped from her grasp and came crashing down on her fingers holding the stake. She screamed and fell back.

"What's wrong," Jennifer shouted

"Just busted my fingers, God it hurts."

Jennifer checked the line

"That should hold, let's get you back inside before we both freeze to death, or drown."

Michelle responded by diving inside and rolling over to her sleeping bag and using the outside of it to dry off before crawling between the zippered bedroll.

Jennifer helped her get back under the dry comfort of the sleeping bag, found a dry shirt and dried Michelle's face and hair the best she could.

"How bad is it?"

"I don't think it's bad, but it hurts like hell right now because it's so cold."

Jennifer climbed in the bag, zipped it and huddled close to her friend for warmth.

"Oh my God, this is miserable," Michelle said shivering against her friend.

"You're telling me. We may be in this tent a lot longer than we wanted to be if this storm keeps up. I was hoping to make it to Mattie's Peak before heading back down the mountain."

"Me too, we'll just have to see what happens in the morning."

***

The storm finally passed. Lightning flashed in the distance, but its fury had burned out and moved on. Steve was sleeping comfortably when he was suddenly awakened. He didn't know if it were a bad dream he was having or a noise outside. He rolled over to his side and closed his eyes to go back to sleep. That's when he heard it.

A thick, low throaty grunt and sniffing just outside the tent. His first thought was a bear had found them. He sat up slowly and quietly trying to not attract its attention.

"Shh," Chris whispered. He was already awake. "Bear. It's been sniffing around for a few minutes now."

Steve nudged his brother to see if he was awake.

"I heard," Mark whispered.

Chris pressed his small derringer into Mark's palm.

"Just in case it tries to get in. I have my .45," Chris said softly.

Steve pushed back the top cover of his sleeping bag being slow and cautious. He didn't want to feel trapped in case it tried to get in. Chris had already done so.

They could hear the animal as it walked near the tent wall. The low, guttural huffing and sniffing were distinctive, but Chris was confused. Even though he was sitting up, he was still relatively close to the ground, the bear seemed to be very tall, well above them.

The animal moved away from the tent. Chris changed positions and began the slow, calculated risk of unzipping the front. Steve reached out to stay his hand, but Chris insisted and pushed ahead. When he the zipper up enough, he pulled back the tent flap to see if he could get a look.

The rain had stopped and moved on, but the erratic wind gusts would blow the tree limbs above the tent. The occupants could hear the large droplets of rainwater fall against the tight weave of the fabric and bounce off. Though the sun wasn't over the horizon yet, the gray, misty morning light provided some visibility.

THE LOST GOLD MINE OF IDAHO SPRINGS

Chris poked his head out and let his eyes adjust. He could hear the footsteps of the bear and knew that it was walking away from the camp. He chanced not alerting the bear to their presence and pulled his boots on. He clambered out trying his best to be stealthy. He pulled the tent flap back and mouthed the words, "*Hold this*" to Steve.

Steve was reluctant and gave Chris a questioning look. "You can't shoot it unless it attacks us," he whispered.

"I'm not," Chris said. "Just want to see if it's gone."

Chris ducked under the opening and stepped into the clearing cautiously peering around. He wrinkled his nose when he caught the same putrid smell from the night before on the wind and motioned to Steve with a wave across his nose. He moved painfully slow, but he didn't want to alert the bear to his presence if he could help it. He held his .45 in an outstretched hand ready to use it if necessary. He had no intention of shooting the bear unless for some reason the bear decided to attack.

The small clearing where the men had made camp was protected on one side by huge boulders and several yards from the forest line on the slope above and below. Chris thought the bear had gone down the mountain judging from the sounds he had heard. He moved over to the firepit they had made and saw that the creature had scattered it out. As he examined the camp, he heard a sound coming from the direction the bear had moved off. He ducked down, spun to face it and brought his sidearm up. He wasn't sure what he was looking at for a moment, all he could see were the trees. Then movement. Very slight, but still movement from something that shouldn't be there. Chris knew not to look directly at the subject, he used his peripheral and let it adjust to it. The bear must be standing on its back legs. It was massive. Chris figured it to be eight or even nine feet tall. The creature had its back to him, so he felt somewhat safe that it hadn't noticed him. He watched the beast for a few seconds, then it moved off into the forest.

"Did you see it?" Mark asked now standing beside him. Steve joined them.

"Yeah, dude that thing was huge!" Chris exclaimed. "I saw it walking off into the woods, but the funny thing is, I think it was walking on its back legs the whole time."

Chris explained what he noticed when the creature was beside the tent.

"Is that typical of a bear? To walk on its hind legs that much?" Mark asked.

"No, it isn't," Steve said. "Bears only walk on their back legs for short periods of time and usually only raise up like that when they feel threatened and want to look big and impressive to another bear or something."

"Still, it was huge. We just need to be careful and not leave any food out. I'm freezing, and I doubt we could get a fire started at all. We should've brought some wood inside to keep it dry overnight or something." Mark said, turning back to the tent and ducking inside.

"I'm right behind ya," Steve said.

After the men were dressed, they had all their gear packed and ready to leave by the time the sun was up over the horizon. They were grateful that the storm came in the night and that they wouldn't have to hike all day in the rain or lose valuable time waiting it out.

"Hey, fellas, check out these tracks," Chris said.

The tracks he spotted were long and wide made by their midnight visitor just outside the tent.

"These don't look like bear tracks. They look almost — human," Mark said kneeling down beside them.

"Nah, can't be. Bears do tend to step into their front tracks with their back paws giving the appearance of a

THE LOST GOLD MINE OF IDAHO SPRINGS

single foot or bipedal. But, this one was strange, I'm telling you that it was walking on its back legs the entire time."

"Okay then genius, explain how it could have stepped into its front tracks if it were walking on its back legs?" Mark said.

"Well, hell, I don't know. Maybe it stood up when it got to the tent."

"I don't know either, but what I do know is, we're losing daylight, and we lost enough of that yesterday," Steve said, casting a mindful glance at Chris.

"Okay, already. Let's get going," Chris said, ignoring the look.

***

Daybreak found the ladies sleeping peacefully in their bright orange and gray tent. Michelle was the first to wake. Her hand ached, but not bad. She examined it the best she could in the dim morning light. There didn't seem to be anything broken, all her fingers worked when she opened and closed her fist, though a bit stiff, only a dull pain that remained. That should work itself out once she was moving.

Jennifer rolled over onto her back. "How is it?" Sensing what her friend was doing.

"It's fine really, just hurts a little, but not bad," Michelle answered in a gravelly morning voice.

"I'd really like to have some Starbucks right now."

"Me too, would you settle for some finely ground, dark, rich and bold Michelle pour over special in a not-so-venti?"

Jennifer laughed. "Perhaps in a short?"

"Yes, a very short collapsible tin cup."

Michelle playfully pushed her friend out of the sleeping bag. After getting dressed, she crawled out of the tent and found the Sterno. She had the small fire going and the portable camp stove around it with water heating a few minutes later while Jennifer started packing the gear.

The sun was shielded behind long, flat sheets of altostratus clouds that allowed just enough sunlight through to let them know it was daytime. Even though it was technically summer, the mountains were cold, especially during the nights with rainy, cloud-covered conditions. The two hikers were experienced and knew how to properly pack for their excursions.

Jennifer had everything packed by the time Michelle had the coffee made. The small camp stove worked perfectly to heat enough water for two small cups of the steaming liquid. The smell alone was comforting.

"Got the bacon and eggs ready yet?" Jennifer asked.

Michelle was vegan, but she knew how her best friend felt about it. Jennifer was one-hundred percent carnivore.

"Sure, come and get it," Michelle laughed.

"Mmm, the coffee certainly smells good. That makes up for having to eat these nasty bars for a week."

"Ah, don't be so glum. Think of it as a flash diet, a cleansing."

Jennifer scoffed. "A Cleansing? Ha! My kind of cleansing involves lots of tequila, Cozumel and a tall, dark and handsome man named Manuel."

Michelle laughed out loud at her friend. Jenni wanted to go to Mexico for a summer vacation, but Michelle had talked her into a more secluded hiking trip to the mountains. The selling point was the cutting-away from the world, the complete stripping of technology and isolation from the city. They both agreed that it would be nice to live without the constant texting and social media.

Jennifer sat on a small rock next to the little camp stove. Looking around she noticed a short stack of rocks not more than twenty feet away.

"Why did you stack those up?"

Michelle followed Jennifer's gaze until she spotted what it was her friend was asking about.

"I didn't do that."

"Then who did? I didn't notice it when we set up camp, and I was walking all around. That's strange."

"I've no idea. I'm sure they've been there for a long time, and we just didn't notice until now. Weird things happen naturally."

Jennifer considered her friend's suggestion, "Yeah, maybe. Just seems – odd really."

Jennifer stood and walked over to the rocks. There were five rocks stacked on top of one another. A Large stone followed by four more each smaller going up. The ground was soaked from the rain, but Jennifer saw a few places where the rocks had been freshly pulled out of the dirt.

"Um, Chelle, these weren't naturally put here like this. Come take a look."

PART VI

"Guys, we've been at this for days now," Chris complained. "There's absolutely nothing out here. We haven't found any of the signs where you say they should be and we're running short on food."

"Yeah, I'm starting to think he's actually right for once," Mark agreed.

Steve stood in a clearing overlooking a small pond, sweat poured down his temple and threatened to sting his eye. He used the back of his hand to wipe it away.

"I know, but somehow I feel like we're close," Steve said, staring off into the distance. "I just know it.

Tomorrow will be a better day. Let's find a place to make camp."

He lingered a moment longer before turning to face them. A quick glance and a shrug of his shoulders, he walked between the two men to continue down the trail. He wasn't ready to give up. Not yet.

Chris traded looks with Mark who shrugged, imitating his older brother, then followed him.

The sun had just gone down as the three men finished pitching their tent, the last of the daylight retiring over the mountain. It took a while to find enough dry wood to build a fire, but they soon had one going well enough to warm up. The heat felt good as they sat quietly waiting on the water to heat up for coffee. Chris took his shoes off and rubbed his feet.

"Look, I'm not saying it's not here. I just think we need a better plan," Chris said, breaking the silence. "What do you say we plan another trip later in the fall? Maybe by then, Steve can dig a little deeper into that journal and figure out why the mine isn't where it's supposed to be."

"I'm not ready to call it quits yet. Let's give it at least another day," Steve said. "I know this is the right area though, I know it!"

Mark stood and looked around. "A hundred and fifty years of weather can change the landscape. At least we know this area a little better now. I mean, that creek you said, the one where the miners worked near the entrance to the cave, it could've dried up, changed course or even went underground. We really have no way of knowing."

"I'm game to give it another day," Chris said.

"Me too. We can get an early start in the morning and make a grid search pattern for the creek. Even if it's dried up and changed course, we should still be able to find the old bed where it ran," Mark suggested.

"Okay, then we're all in agreement. We give it one more day. Then, if nothing turns up, we head home and make another plan to come back in a few weeks," Steve said.

"Now that that's settled, how about getting some sleep, I'm freakin' exhausted," Mark said.

The morning came quickly, along with a fierce wind. Steve was the first to wake. He lay in his sleeping bag and listened to the wind howling across the ravine less than a hundred yards from the camp. Each gust shook the small red and black tent, but the stakes held firm. The other two men were still sleeping, he could hear them snoring. He rolled onto his back and stared at the ceiling and watched the ripples as the structure danced in the wind. The dim light of daybreak filtered through the window.

The gold mine kept sleep at bay. He lay awake most of the night thinking about it. It wasn't necessarily the thought of gold that drove him, it was the thought of piecing together all the clues that were over a hundred and fifty years old and finding the mine. The find itself is what propelled him. *I know we're close to it, I just know it*, he thought. He sat up and stretched accompanied by a huge, sleepy yawn. *Where did I go wrong? The clues are all right there in the journal. The creek could've changed course over the years as Mark suggested, but the dried-up creek bed would still be there, but it's not where I thought it would be.*

He couldn't lie idle any longer. He slipped on his clothes and boots and scrambled out of the tent eager to get started. Poking at last night's firepit remains, he found a few coals and had a warm blaze going in no time.

A weird sensation suddenly came over him causing the hair on his neck to stand as if he were being watched.

"Thinking about that gold mine aren't ya?" Chris asked, startling his friend. He had woken and slipped out of the tent without Steve noticing.

"Yeah, dude, I know we're close. I can feel it."

"Damn, it's windy. You got the coffee going yet?"

"Working on it. Yeah, this wind kept me awake most of the night. I pretty much dozed off and on."

"Sure wish you two would clam up out there, I'm trying to get my beauty sleep up in here," Mark half shouted from the tent.

"If anyone needs their beauty sleep, it's damn well going to be you, but honestly, if you slept for a hundred years it wouldn't help your ugly ass," Chris said.

"Very funny. What time is it?" Mark asked as he ducked out of the tent rubbing his eyes.

Steve looked at his watch. "Time to get up and moving."

Three trail-bars, two cups of coffee and a half an hour later the three men were back on the trail in their search for signs of the gold mine.

***

"We never should've left the trail, and now we've been doing nothing, but walking around in circles all day. We're practically out of food, I'm exhausted, and I just want to go home. Face it, we're lost," Chris complained.

Steve turned and looked over his shoulder at his brother, a heavy sigh escaped his lips.

"Yeah, I know. Trust me, I know. We lost the map," Steve said looking at Chris before shifting his gaze to Mark who was sitting on a rock rubbing a sprained ankle. "Now the Garmin is toast, so I think the best thing we can do is try to back-track our way out."

"We could be out here for days, weeks even, and no one would ever find us," Chris chimed. "We'll starve to death first."

The Turner brothers turned and glared at Chris.

"I thought you were a tracking expert," Mark said.

"I am, I can track just about anything, but after the storm this morning, any signs of our passing have all been washed away. Face it, fellas, we're gonna die."

"Seriously, Chris, shut up," Steve said. "Let's get moving. We need to get Mark down and a warm fire going so he can rest until that ankle is better. Once we find a way down to the bottom of this ravine, then we can follow the mountain runoff to the bottom. Surely, we'll come across a road or a trail, something."

"I'm sorry I cut our trip short you guys, this totally blows," Mark apologized.

"We just have to remember to bring a backup GPS next time," Steve said.

"And a map," Chris chimed in.

"Hey, wait! Look over there, is that people?" Steve said.

***

Michelle stopped suddenly and held her hand up for silence.

"What is it?"

"Shh," Michelle hushed, motioning for her friend to listen. She thought she heard something and strained to listen.

A few minutes later, she turned and shrugged. "Eh, guess it was nothing."

"What'd you think it was?"

"I could've sworn I heard someone shouting. Sounded like a man."

Jennifer laughed. "I've been telling you if you don't find a man soon, people are going to start thinking you play for the other team."

"Ha-ha, aren't you funny?" Michelle deadpanned. "Just remember this, it would be years, *if ever*, that anyone finds your body out here."

"Shhhh."

This time it was Jennifer that heard it. The trail they traveled ran alongside a vast ravine that dropped down several hundred feet, and equally expansive across. The wind blew over the mountain and came across the chasm, picking up speed and whipping against the side where they stood in a constant gale. Sounds swirled on the wind, like autumn leaves of Maple trees scattering across a lawn. There was no way of knowing which direction the sound came from.

"I heard it too," Michelle whispered, holding her hand up to remain quiet. "There it is again!"

"Yeah, no mistake about it. That's a man shouting. Where's it coming from?"

"There! Look, on the other side," Jennifer said, pointing across the ravine.

Two people stood waving to the ladies on the other side about halfway down. It was more than a few football fields across, so they were hard to see at first glance and with the wind blowing so hard, they could barely hear them yelling.

Michelle quickly dropped her pack and pulled out a bright colored t-shirt and waved it high overhead.

"Are you okay?" she shouted, but it was no use. He couldn't hear her, but she knew he was in trouble. It would take a few hours to get down the ravine and back up to where he was. She held her hands up to indicate they should stay put. "Stay there," she shouted when the wind died down for a brief second. "We're coming to you."

Nearly three hours later, the two girls reached the bottom of the ravine. There was no fast or safe way down

THE LOST GOLD MINE OF IDAHO SPRINGS

and across, and the going was slow. A small creek lay at the bottom, but there were plenty of large boulders and downed trees that enabled them to cross. Once over, it didn't take them long to reach the area where they thought the stranded hikers were.

"I don't see them now?" Michelle said, looking around.

"Hello!" Jennifer shouted.

"Up here," they heard a man's voice yell.

They hurried up the slope, climbing over dead trees and rocks. When the girls arrived, they saw there were three men, not two like they thought.

"Thank God you heard us. We got lost and were on the way back down the mountain when Mark here fell on the rocks, twisted his ankle pretty bad."

"It hurts, but I don't think it's broken," Jennifer said, kneeling beside Mark.

"What happened?"

Steve pointed at Mark, who leaned back on his elbows, his legs outstretched in front. "As embarrassing as it is," he began, but Chris cut him off.

"We were on our way back to the campgrounds at Mist Falls," he said, pointing in the direction they were traveling. "That's when Mark fell and twisted his ankle. That's all."

The girls both looked at Chris. They knew there was more to the story, but chose to say nothing now.

"Can you walk at all?" Jennifer asked, turning to Mark.

He sat up and gingerly rubbed his ankle. "With a little help, I can."

"It'll be dark soon," Michell said. "We should to get him down to the bottom and make camp near the creek."

"Yeah, there's no way we're getting off this mountain in the dark," Jennifer said.

"Let's get him on his feet and get moving."

Once they reached the bottom of the ravine, the group

quickly set about getting the camp set up for the night. Michelle helped Steve gather dead tree limbs and built a fire. There was a natural spring nearby to help make some coffee. The sun went down, leaving the night pitch black. The wind settled, blowing in storm clouds and blotting out the moon and the stars, making the night even darker. The rain held off, but lightning flashed off in the distance. There was a good chance they would be hiking off the mountain the next day in the rain. Mark sat near the fire, holding a small cup of coffee when Jennifer sat down. "How's the ankle?"

"It's better. I'm sure it'll be fairly stiff in the morning, but I should be able to put some weight on it."

"That's good. So, what are you guys doing out here?"

Mark turned back to the fire and used a stick to poke at the burning wood, sending tiny embers floating. "Just camping, you know, getting away for a few days."

"When we were up on the hill, your friend said you were heading back to the campgrounds at Mist Falls."

Mark said nothing, just nodded and continued poking at the fire.

"Trouble is," Michelle said, joining the conversation. "Your friends could've helped you down here. You didn't need us. Not to mention, the direction you were heading isn't anywhere near the direction of Mist Falls."

"It's okay, Mark," Steve said. "You can tell 'em." Chris walked over and sat down beside his brother.

Jennifer traded looks with Michelle.

"Truth is, we're lost."

"We're not lost," Chris said.

"Don't listen to him, he's an idiot. Yes, we are lost. We've been out here running around looking for a lost gold mine for the last three days, and got turned around."

"A lost gold mine? Really?" Jennifer asked.

"Yeah," Mark said. "Steve here believes there's a lost gold mine somewhere out here. He found a book in a yard sale that he believes tells of its location."

"It's not a book, it's a handwritten journal."

"Yeah, yeah, whatever. I think you're still nuts."

"So, where are you from?" Michelle asked.

"Idaho Springs," Steve answered.

"Oh, okay, Clear Creek, I should've known," Michelle laughed. "We're from Golden."

Before Steve could ask what she meant by her comment, he was cut off by his brother.

"Seriously," Mark said. "If you two hadn't come along when you did, who knows if we would have found our way out. You *do* know the way out, right?"

Michelle hesitated a moment. Unable to hold back any longer, she laughed. "Yeah, we know our way down. We parked at Mist Falls too, and we hike here all the time. That's why when we saw you on the other side of the ravine, we knew something was up. It's only a day's hike out so, yeah, we can save you."

They all enjoyed a good laugh.

"Is there any coffee left or did you drink it all?" Steve asked.

PART VII

Michelle was the first to wake the next morning. She unzipped the tent and slipped out, careful not to wake Jennifer. The fire went out sometime during the night, but she added more wood to the coals and soon had it blazing again. The heat felt good and knocked the chill off the early morning. The storm clouds remained, blocking the sunlight and leaving the woods in a gray hue.

"Good morning," Steve said, his voice low and ragged.

Michelle spun. "I didn't notice you get up. Scared me."

"Sorry."

"No worries, I was just about to make some coffee. Want some?"

"Sounds good. I'll give you a hand."

The smell alone was eye-opening, but Steve felt much better after the first sip of the freshly brewed coffee. He sat across from Michelle and tossed another small dead limb on the fire.

"The others will smell it and be up soon I'm sure," he said.

"I bet so. Hey so, I'm curious, do you mind me asking about this lost gold mine? Is that for real or was it just a joke to hide the fact that you guys got lost and two women had to save you?"

"Ha, very funny," Steve laughed. "I suppose it won't hurt to tell you."

Michelle listened closely as Steve told her the story of the lost gold mine. Before he finished, the others had woke, poured coffee for themselves and listened quietly.

"I'm guessing you never found any sign of it though, or you wouldn't be leaving," Jennifer said.

"No, we didn't, but I know we're close," Steve said.

"I don't believe it really exists," Chris said.

Steve shot him a nasty look.

"What? What I'd say?"

"Oh, ye of little faith," Steve chided. "It's out there, I know it is. I just have to do a little more research. The weather here in the mountains can be drastic and can change the lay of the land over the course of a hundred and fifty years you know."

"I understand that, but for all we know that cave or mine, or whatever has been caved in for years from rock

THE LOST GOLD MINE OF IDAHO SPRINGS

slides or avalanche, we may never find it."

"Chris could be right," Jennifer added.

"Maybe, but I'm still going to try to find it," Steve said. "I'll come back alone if I have to."

"Would you mind if I looked at the journal?" Michelle offered. "Maybe I can help. I've been hiking this mountain ever since I was a little girl. My family comes here to camp and hike all the time."

"Sure, I don't mind at all." Steve hurried to get the journal and his notes out of his pack and returned a moment later.

"While you two look over that stuff, we'll get packed up," Chris said.

Michelle took the journal and read through it and referenced Steve's notes.

"Steve, let me ask you something. There's a reference to a creek they had to cross made from mountain runoff of two mountain peaks, one being half the size of the other. They crossed just below where they joined. From what I can gather, mind you the journal is faded in areas, there was a pool where they were able to stop and make camp."

"Yeah, and there's another place later where he mentions the pool again," Steve said. "Something about standing under the waterfall. That part is hard to make out. Just too faded, but I think that the two mountain streams probably joined together and cascaded over rocks that made the waterfall. I think they crossed below all of that because the fast-moving water of the falls was probably slowed down by the pool before running over and on down the mountain. Does that make sense?"

"Actually, it makes perfect sense. I think I know where that is."

"Seriously?"

"Yeah, but it doesn't look like that now, of course.

Several years ago, loggers built a road back in that area. The road didn't last long because of all the rock and mudslides. It was abandoned after a few years, and the loggers made new roads on the other side of the mountain. I remember my dad telling me about it. I've only been through there once maybe, but I remember it. I'm more than certain that's where they crossed."

Mark limped over and sat down next to Michelle. "Okay, say that is the place they crossed, that still doesn't tell us where they went after that, does it?"

"It doesn't, but the journal talks about once they made it to the other side of the creek the going got much easier. They climbed the mountain following the runoff of the smaller peak. They neared the top and then moved westward along a ridge. That's when they found the valley. Made camp in the meadow near a clear mountain pool. His writing is very poetic. People just don't talk like that these days. That's when they discovered a hole in the ground that turned out to be a cave. *The* cave."

"I read that part. Apparently, over the next few days is when they discovered the gold, but that's also when something started happening. The missing pages sure could help explain what happened, but I take it they were attacked. Whether it was by other prospectors, Indians or animals, it doesn't say. It's a mystery."

"He made mention that during the crossing, they lost a few of their supplies that weren't tied down good on one of their mules. They found the pack that fell off later, but there was nothing left as the animals must've made a feast of it. When they found it, it was torn to shreds, and all the goods were gone. It could've been bears or mountain lions."

Michelle stood suddenly. "Could be. Is anyone in a hurry to get back home?"

Everyone said no or shook their heads.

"Why?" Steve asked.

"Well, depending on how Mark's ankle feels in the morning, I'm sure that I can guide us to that spot!!"

***

The hike up the mountain to the area where Michelle thought could be the trail of the miners didn't take long. By early afternoon most of the clouds had moved out and the sun shined brightly, raising the temperature. The group stood on what looked to be the old logging road. Following the path, they came to an area that had been washed out and was forced to skirt around it. The underbrush was thick but manageable.

"We're pretty close now. Shouldn't be more than a half hour's walk from here to the place where the two mountain flows came together," Michelle said, stopping to wipe away the sweat from her forehead.

"I sure hope you can find your way back. It's like canopy jungle up in here," Chris said.

"Oh, quit worrying ya big baby," Mark quipped.

"I'm not worried. Besides, I'm part Cherokee, I can find my way out."

Steve scoffed, "Right, need I remind your dumbass that before these two ladies came along, we were *LOST*?"

"No, we weren't. I had it under control."

Steve laughed, "What direction are we facing now?"

Chris stopped walking and looked around. "That way is west, so we are traveling due north."

"I rest my case. Chris – you're an idiot," Steve said, shoving Chris out of the way and moving forward.

"What was that for? What'd I say?"

Michelle and Jennifer laughed at the exchange and

followed Steve over the rocks.

Mark shot Chris a look of feigned disgust and shook his head in disbelief, "If we depended on you to find our way out of these mountains, we would all die. Whoever told you the sun sits in the north? Dumbass!"

***

"Wow, look at that," Jennifer said.

The group came to the edge of a cliff to look down into a beautiful scene below. A small stream cascaded down step-stone rocks to splash into a crystal-clear pool surrounded by lush, green foliage. A meadow filled with tall, golden-brown grass waved in the breeze that flowed over the mountain, changing directions like a school of fish. Thick, green cattails grew around the edge of the other side of the pool.

"Incredible. It's beautiful. Look at the water falling over the rocks. I bet you could stand under it," Steve said. "Wow!"

"Wow, is right. That's awesome. Completely undisturbed by man, purely natural. I'd love to build a small cabin right there in the middle of that field," Chris said.

Steve didn't miss a beat, "Then it would be disturbed, and it would look like your old truck in no time. Beer cans laying all around, empty tv dinner trays mixed in for good measure and, of course, an engine hanging from a tree."

"What is this, pick on Chris day?"

"Well, you do ask for it sometimes."

"That's enough you guys," Jennifer said. "Let's get down there and check it out."

"Definitely. I bet that's the place that they talked about in the journal," Steve chimed in.

"That's what I'm thinking too," Michelle said. "I

remember this place from years ago. My parents used to bring the family to the mountains to camp. Our dog ran off and got lost, and we searched for him for two days. My dad found this place then. I've not been back since but had always wanted to find it again. Hikers don't come here because it's too far from the trails and I don't think anyone knows about it."

The group backtracked the way they came for a short distance before cutting back through the woods until they arrived at the runoff. They crossed the fast-moving stream over large boulders in the middle of it and followed its path back up toward the pool in single file.

Michelle led the way, her yellow and orange backpack stuck up above her head moving slightly up and down with each step. Wearing khaki shorts, a blue t-shirt, and hiking shoes, her longs legs were naturally tanned from the summer sun. Steve couldn't help but notice as he followed closely behind. She was strong, smart and capable with a confidence about her that Steve found attractive.

"You said you're from Golden, right?" Steve asked.

"Yup, born and raised."

"A Demon huh? That's cool. We have family that lives there," Steve said, doing his best not to sound nervous. Idle chit-chat wasn't his specialty when it came to the opposite sex.

"Yeah, Jenni and I grew up together there. Been best friends since we could walk."

"You made a comment yesterday when I told you we are from Idaho Springs. What was that about?"

Michelle laughed, "You also said that you were looking for a lost gold mine. Isn't the Clear Creek High School mascot the Gold Diggers?"

"Damn, never thought about that," Steve laughed.

The trail beside the stream was skirted by the tall grass

and was well worn. The hikers saw several tracks of different animals along the way but saw no indication that the animals were still there. Elk tracks mixed with lots of deer made up the bulk of what they saw. When they parted the grass and entered the clearing near the pool, they all stopped in their tracks. Standing on the far bank, a doe with two yearlings were drinking the cold mountain water. The hikers watched for a few minutes in silence so as not to spook them. The mother, ever diligent in her protective watch, however, knew something was off and quickly moved the two youngsters out of the area.

"It's even more beautiful down here," Jennifer said. She moved past the group and dropped her backpack down near the pool. Dropping to her knees, she leaned down and cupped her hands under the overflow and took a drink. "Amazing. Tastes better than Fuji."

The others quickly joined her. Mark slid his pack down off his shoulders and pulled the water bottle out. His ankle was a bit stiff, but he wasn't in pain. He knew he had slowed the others down, but there was nothing he could do about that now. They all made the decision to search for the mine knowing all the variables. He issued a lengthy sigh that seemed to come from far away. He was tired.

"It's already getting kinda late in the day, maybe we should get the camp set up?" Mark suggested.

"Yeah, I agree," Michelle replied. "We may have enough time to explore before it gets too dark."

"I hate to say this, but I absolutely have to be back at work on Tuesday," Jennifer said.

"I hear ya. I have to be back on Monday, so if we don't find anything by tomorrow, we may be out of luck," Steve said.

"Let's grab something to eat and get camp set up. After that we should have a little time to explore," Steve suggested.

"Good idea," Jennifer said. "I'm starving. Haven't had anything since the energy bar earlier today. What I wouldn't give for something different right now!"

Chris, who had moved off to explore the pool, overheard Jennifer. "How about a nice, fresh salad?" He asked.

"There he goes again," Mark said.

"That would be wonderful," Jennifer said. "But, I don't think we can get delivery out here in the middle of nowhere."

"I'll admit, I don't have any raspberry vinaigrette dressing, but I have the greens," Chris said smiling.

The others walked over near him for an explanation.

"This cattail has everything we need. They're actually nutritious and don't taste half bad."

"What, pray tell, is cattail?" Michelle asked.

"This," Chris said as he pulled one of the tall green stalks out of the pool. "The lower parts of the leaves can be eaten raw. You can make a salad out of it. There's actually a lot of different ways to use it. This yellow pollen can be added to soups and stews or mix it with flour for bread. The roots can be dried and ground up to make flour too, lots of protein."

"I've never heard of cattail," Jennifer admitted.

"It's also called Bulrush," Chris said, breaking a few leaves off and munching on it. He handed some to the girls.

"Now, that, I've heard of," Michelle said, taking a bite of the green leaf. "I have to say, it's not bad."

"Look at you Mr. Survivalist," Jennifer laughed.
Chris smiled, "I'll take that as a compliment."

A short time later, after the two tents were up and a fire pit made in the center, the group split up to explore.

Making their way along the banks of the pool, Steve and Michelle headed for the waterfall. The cold, crystal clear mountain water glimmered even in the fading light of the early summer evening. Huge boulders, broken and splintered by thousands of years of natural erosion formed a long oval pool where snowmelt from the two mountain peaks crashed down a path of least resistance. The deep pool only gave pause, a slight hesitation in the incremental cascade as it joined with other runoff streams, forming a roaring river far below. The break, however, seemed almost divinely inspired as its perfect timing alongside the beautiful, peaceful valley filled with tall, graceful grasses and scattered gray-barked Birch trees. The entire scene, majestic, wild and untamed, was a complete work of art, a masterpiece painted by the greatest master of them all.

The intrepid explorers climbed the layered rocks to the top of the falls. From there, they could see much of the valley below. A bowl-shaped arroyo formed below the two mountain peaks and stretched strategically from the rising sun of the east to the western horizon almost as if by design. Aligned perfectly to catch all the day's radiance for a perfect balance of vegetation. Scattered across the valley floor grew Mountain Harebells and beautiful bright blue and purple Alpine Forget-Me-Nots. Standing on the rocks, they could feel the power of the water as it flowed over the twenty-foot fall and crashed with all the force of a locomotive into the pool below.

"Let's cross over on those rocks and look around on the other side," Steve suggested.

"I'll let you lead the way," Michelle laughed. "I like my water frozen."

"A skier huh?"

"Snowboarding's my thing. Every chance I get. What about you?"

THE LOST GOLD MINE OF IDAHO SPRINGS

"I ski, sort of. Guess you can call it that," he laughed, leaping from one large, flat rock to another one. "I'm just not that athletically inclined, I suppose. Your turn."

She took a quick-step run and leaped across the four-foot span with ease. There were several large rocks scattered across the stream that allowed them to get across safely. Once on the other side, they clambered down the edge to the base of the falls. The misty spray of the falls was thick and soaked their clothes quickly.

"Well, we're wet now. Might as well keep going," Steve said, smiling at her. He smoothed back the dark brown hair out of his eyes.

Michelle laughed at him. Her hair, also wet, stuck to her forehead and covered her eyes. Dozens of tiny water droplets clung to her face until the moisture collected too much water and finally slid down her suntanned bronze skin. Her chest heaved from the sudden exertion of scurrying over and under the rocks and the frigid, rapid flow of melted ice and snow.

"Oh my God, it's cold in here," she said.

"You're telling me. I really didn't think it would be this cold. You could store meat in here."

They stood at the edge of a fissure directly behind the sheets of falling water. The freshly melted snow from high on the peaks poured down the mountainside and emptied into lakes and rivers below. The power of the flows created pockets in the rocks like the one they stood in now. What little daylight was left allowed them to see only a few feet into the cave.

"I wish I had brought my flashlight with me."

"Yeah, me too," Michelle said, clinging to Steve's arm as they inched their way further in. "Not much sunlight left. We'll have to come back tomorrow and check it out." Her voice echoed off the cave walls.

Steve held his arm out in front of him to feel his way around and shuffled his feet to inch further inside. "Hello!" His voice, bouncing off the solid rock walls replied with an eerie, rapid echo.

"That's cool, but I don't think we should go any further. I can't feel where I'm at, and I dang sure don't want to fall into a bottomless pit."

Michelle groaned, "Ugh, that would be bad. When we come back, remind me to bring a can of Febreze, this place sure has a nasty funk to it."

"Agreed!" Steve laughed. "Probably a mixture of dead fish and decaying carcasses from beavers or something. It is a bit – rank."

As darkness began closing in on the hidden valley, the spelunkers meandered back to camp and joined Mark and Jennifer around the fire they had built earlier. They changed out of their wet clothes and lay the wet things near the heat to dry.

"What happened to you two? Go for a swim?" Mark asked.

Michelle sat down as close to the fire as she could. Her body still shaking from the cold. "Not a chance. That's ice water. We found a cave entrance beneath the falls. Not sure how far it goes back, but the echoes of our voices made it sound huge, didn't have a flashlight though so, we couldn't explore it."

Steve chimed in, "Yeah, dude, we've got to go check it out tomorrow."

"Cool, I'm game. Maybe that's where the gold mine is?" Chris said, plopping down near the fire and leaned on his elbow to one side. He immediately winced in pain.

"Rock?" Jennifer asked.

"Must be," he answered. He sat up and dug into the ground. A few minutes later he held up an object that

THE LOST GOLD MINE OF IDAHO SPRINGS

seemed to be made of iron.

"What is it?" Michelle asked.

"Not sure," Chris said, examining the object closely. "Looks like something that may go on a harness for horses maybe."

"Or pack mules," Steve said. "Can I see that?"

Chris handed him the metal object consisting of an iron ring attached to a dried out, brittle piece of leather.

"Yeah, I'm sure of it. This looks like a piece of a harness for pack horses or mules or something. What else could it be? This has to be the place. No doubt in my mind," Steve said.

"Okay, that's freaking awesome," Mark said. "That mine has to be close then. Too bad it's dark now, or I'd say let's get going!"

"Speaking of that, where's my flashlight? Jenni, do you mind coming with me to the little girls' tree?" Michelle asked.

The girls took their flashlights and left the camp. The tall grass swayed gently in the evening breeze making a swishing sound each time a gust picked up. Owls hooted in the night in search of meals and bullfrogs croaked nearby. No stars lit the way, the only light came from the small flashlights they each carried.

PART VIII

"I think I'm turning in as soon as they get back," Steve said. "I'm exhausted. Doubt I can sleep though. Too pumped up about the gold mine. The journal talked about everything we've found so far – the crossing point, the valley, the waterfall, and cave, it's gotta be close!"

"I hear ya. I guess I may finally believe you now," Chris

said.

***

Jenni followed her friend through the tall grass until they came to a small clearing near a large tree.

"I can't believe just how dark it can be out here," Jennifer said.

"I know, it's a little eerie."

"A little?" Michelle chuckled. "This place, as beautiful as it is in the daylight, is equally as spooky at night."

"What was that?" Michelle said, spinning around with her flashlight.

"What is it? What'd you see?"

"Heard something. Hey, who's there? This isn't funny you guys?" Michelle said.

A grunting sound came from somewhere in the darkness followed by a loud 'whooping' noise.

"We are not amused, you guys. This isn't funny at all," Michelle shouted.

Suddenly, a large rock landed just a few feet away from the girls and rolled near their feet.

"Oh my God," Jenni said, grabbing Michelle's arm.

"Leave us alone," Michelle shouted.

The girls shined their flashlights, searching for any sign of the unwanted guests. The grass was four to five feet tall, and they couldn't see but a few feet around them. A towering figure loomed up from the grass standing at least eight feet tall. They knew immediately, it wasn't the men. Jennifer dropped her flashlight as panicked overtook her. A shout froze in her throat. Michelle screamed. A high-pitched, fear-filled scream. She grabbed Jenni's arm, spun her away from the hulking figure, and ran.

THE LOST GOLD MINE OF IDAHO SPRINGS

***

The fire had burned low. Steve added a few more sticks of dry wood to make sure there would be adequate coals for in the morning. He couldn't survive without his morning coffee. Hopefully, the rain would hold off, but the storm clouds from earlier weren't promising.

Mark stared silently into the flames as the fire danced in the darkness. Tiny embers floated on the gentle breeze and burned themselves out within seconds. Suddenly, the solitude of the quiet evening was shaken into chaos as screams from what had to be Jennifer and Michelle pierced the night. The men jumped to their feet in an instant and searched the darkness in the direction of the screams.

"Where are they?" Chris asked.

"There," Mark pointed. "I saw the flash of light."

Steve was already moving with his small flashlight in hand.

"Wait up," Mark said. "I'm right behind you."

Chris ran into the tent, grabbed his backpack and located his pistol. He was only seconds behind the brothers.

"Where are you?" Steve shouted. He could hear the girls panicked screaming. They were on the move, running from something. Mark reached his side.

"Anything?"

"No, I lost 'em," Steve said. "Not sure which way they went."

Chris reached the brothers, flashlight in one hand and pistol in the other. "Anything?" he asked.

"Nothing," Steve said. "The last I heard, I think they were running in that direction. This grass is so damn tall!"

"Tell me about it, I could hear you hollering, but I couldn't even see your flashlights," Chris complained.

As suddenly as the shouting began, the evening fell into

an eerie silence. The three men stood silent, looking in all directions for any sign of the girl's flashlights or voices.

"Let's head in that direction then,"

"Mark, maybe you should head back to camp and wait there in case they come back. I can see that ankle is still bothering you," Steve suggested.

"I'm good, I can keep up."

"No, you really can't. You'll slow us down. Besides, what if you step on it wrong out here in the dark? We'll have to carry your ass back. Not happening. Just wait for us at the camp."

Mark knew his brother was right. Any misstep out here and he could do worse damage to the ankle and be of no use to anyone.

"Okay, I'll build a fire up as high as I can. If you get turned around, head to the high ground and look for it."

"Sounds good," Steve said. "Let's get going, Chris."

***

A limb slapped back and hit Jennifer in the face as the girls raced through the darkness trying to allude whatever was chasing them. She didn't notice as fear-infused adrenaline coursed through her veins. They could hear the weight of the beast as it ran after them. Whatever it was chasing them, it was for sure not a person.

They raced through the tall grass as quickly as they could, but there was no way of knowing which direction the campsite was now. They were not tall enough to see the glow of the fire. They found a narrow path that led into the woods. Thinking it would be easier going, they took it and picked up the pace.

"Is it still following us," Michelle asked. "What was it? A bear?"

"Can't tell. I don't hear it anymore. Turn off the light," Jennifer panted.

They heard nothing except their own breathing as they stood in silence in the darkness. Whatever had been chasing them seemed to have stopped, for the moment.

"What's that?" Jennifer whispered.

"Sounded like Steve."

They listened carefully, straining to hear which direction he may be.

"There, that's definitely Steve," Michelle said. "But, I don't see where he is."

"Oh my God, look!" Jennifer said, pointing in the distance. It was the campfire.

PART X

Mark gathered more wood for the fire and built it as high as he could. When he was done, the bonfire was blazing at least ten feet into the night sky. When he was satisfied, he gathered as much wood as he could to keep it going. There wasn't much dead wood remaining in the area. He hoped the group would be able to see it and make their way back as soon as possible.

He leaned down to pick up a large branch when he heard a loud, *whoop, whoop* coming from nearby in the darkness.

"Who's there?" He shouted.

A huge, hulking figure suddenly raised up above the tall grass just before him. Mark shined his flashlight into the face of a fierce looking beast of the likes he had never seen before. He froze in fear as the creature glared at him. He turned and ran back to the fire, his heart racing much faster than his feet.

***

Chris shouted, "Michelle, Jennifer, where are you?"

"Hey, turn your light off a second," Steve said. "Look! Over there."

The glow of a flashlight lying on the ground could be seen just a few feet away.

"This has to be theirs," Chris said, as he picked it up.

"Which way did they go?" Steve mused. "Ground's too hard to pick out any tracks, especially in the dark."

"If I had to guess, I'd… Oof!" Something hit Chris from behind knocking him to the ground.

"Chris!" Steve shouted. He saw the huge limb that struck his friend. Someone had thrown it from behind them. He reached down and helped his buddy to his feet. "Let's go!" He shouted.

The two were on their feet and on the run through the head high grass. Another massive figure suddenly appeared in front of them. A blood-curdling scream from the creature stopped them two men in their tracks. Chris brought the pistol up instinctively and fired three shots at the beast. He heard it yelp in pain before Steve pulled him in the opposite direction.

"Run!" Steve yelled.

***

Michelle whispered into Jenni's ear, "Let's leave the flashlight off and head towards the fire."

"We can't walk around out here in the dark. We can't see anything," Jennifer whispered.

"We have to try," Michelle said. "I'm not standing out here to be eaten by a frikkin' bear!"

THE LOST GOLD MINE OF IDAHO SPRINGS

***

Steve felt the ground disappear beneath his feet.

"Oomph!" He fell straight down and hit with a hard thud against the dirt-floor of an underground cave entrance. Chris, following closely behind him, was unable to stop in time and fell on top of him.

"Are you okay?" Chris asked.

"Yeah, yeah, I think so," Steve finally responded. "Nothing seems broken anyway."

"Do you still have your flashlight? I dropped mine, and it must've gone out," Chris asked. "I've gotta find my gun. I dropped it too when I hit. Thanks for breaking my fall by the way."

"Glad I could help! No, I dropped mine too. Let's feel around, maybe we can find one of 'em and figure out where we are before that damn thing finds us. What the hell is it?"

"I don't know, but I know I hit it. At least once anyway. I heard it holler when I shot at it."

Steve scrambled to his hands and knees and felt his way around. "Found your gun," he reported.

"Hey, that's something!" Chris whispered. "I feel a hell of a lot better now."

"I'd feel a lot better if we had at least one flashlight to see with. I don't want you shooting me!"

"Here it is," Chris said, turning on the flashlight. He put a finger over the end of it to keep the beam small as not to be seen by the animal chasing them.

"We need to get out of here and find those girls before that damn thing does!"

"What is that thing? A bear?"

"That wasn't a damn bear dude! I don't know what the hell it is, but that's not a frikkin' bear!"

"Then what the hell is it?"

"Whatever it is, it's flesh and blood, and that means it can die!"

"Where are we anyway?" Steve asked.

"Not sure, but it looks like it goes back a ways, but we don't have time to explore it now. Not if we want to live!"

"Hey, shine that light over here again," Steve said.

Chris turned the light over to where Steve indicated. Shoots of gold surrounded by milky quartz gangue shined in the bright LED light on the cave wall.

"Holy Hell! We found it!"

"Yeah, but we also found why those miners got the hell out and never came back!" Steve said.

"Okay, what do we do now?" Chris asked.

"We get out of here, find the girls and get them back to camp."

"How do we find them?"

"I'm hoping that when you shot the damn thing, it ran off. Let's get going."

The two men climbed out of the cave opening which was only about five feet below the surface. They were careful to listen for any sign that the beast could still be lingering, but once they were satisfied it was gone, they backtracked the way they came.

"Damn, that's a hell of a fire he's got going on," Chris said when he noticed the blaze a few hundred yards away.

"I'll say. Surely the girls will see it too and make for it!"

No sooner had he said that when they heard a rustling in the field coming from behind them.

"When it gets closer, turn the flashlight on and light it up! I'll blow his ass away," Chris whispered.

They hunkered down in the tall grass and waited. The sounds of something making its way through the grass grew louder with each waiting second. Just as they were about to jump up and surprise the beast, a flashlight beam flashed on the ground in front of them.

"Don't shoot," Steve whispered. He stood and turned his own light on. It was Michelle and Jennifer.

"Oh my God, are we glad to see you," Michelle said.

"Did you see what it was?" Chris asked.

"No, not exactly," Jennifer said, trembling.

"I saw it," Michelle said. "It wasn't a bear, but it was just as big if not bigger!"

"I don't care what the son of a bitch is, let's get back to camp. Mark's alone there, and he's all gimped up," Steve said. "Chris, you have the gun, lead the way."

***

Mark grabbed the longest branch he could find in the fire. Whatever that thing was that was chasing him might be afraid of the flames. He could feel the beast moving right behind him. He turned and waved it menacingly at the massive creature. He was right, the creature was afraid of the fire and retreated into the darkness. It screamed furiously but ran away.

***

Chris led the way back to the camp in single file with Steve bringing up the rear. He kept the flashlight beam as small as possible in his left hand and the pistol at the ready in the other. The group held one hand on the person in front of them and moved along steadily. Chris stopped the group several times to listen for any signs the beast could be close, but when hearing nothing, they continued. The camp was less than a hundred yards away.

Jennifer stumbled and fell forward into Michelle's legs

knocking them both to the ground in a tangled mess, almost taking Chris with them.

"Ow!" Michelle said falling to the ground. Her elbow landed hard on a rock. Rolling onto her bottom, she sat up rubbing it gingerly

"Sorry Chelle," Jennifer whispered. "I tripped over a rock or something."

"I'm alright. Let's just get going."

"Shh, don't move," Chris whispered, clicking off the flashlight. "Something's following us."

Steve heard something as well and felt around for anything to use as a weapon. A large rock was all he could find. Adrenaline pumped through his system. He was scared.

Chris eased around the girls as quietly as he could and waited with Steve. Whatever was following them stopped whenever they stopped.

"Let's force it out," Chris whispered. "When we do, the girls can run back to camp, and I'll shoot it. I have fourteen rounds of .45 left. I don't care what it is, it can't live filled with lead."

"I'm game," Steve said.

"Okay, as soon as we jump up and run at it, you two run as fast as you can back to camp. We're gonna end this thing," Chris explained to the girls.

They understood and made ready to run.

Chris gave the signal. The girls bolted for the camp. He and Steve stood, screaming as loudly as they could, trying to be as intimidating as possible to their adversary. The beast stood and rushed at them. It was massive. Chris was ready and fired several shots. The creature fell within a few yards of the men.

"Let's go!" Chris shouted.

They bolted for the camp not far behind the girls. An

enraged scream pierced the night from somewhere in the middle of the tall grass. Chris held onto the firearm as tightly as possible. If he fell, he couldn't afford to drop it again.

The two men arrived at the camp moments after the girls. Mark had the fire roaring with huge logs.

"What the hell are those things and how goddamn many are there?" Mark asked.

"I don't know, but they're not bears!" Steve shouted. "We need more fire. Spread it all around us. Maybe it will keep them away."

"One of 'em attacked me here at the camp, but when I shoved fire in its face it backed off!" Mark said.

"We gotta get out of here," Jennifer cried.

"There's no way we can make it out of these mountains at night," Steve said.

Lightning flashed several times, and thunder shook the valley.

"Are you fucking kidding me?" Chris yelled, ducking into the tent to search for his pack.

The rain began slowly at first, but within seconds had picked up, falling hard and pelting the campers. They watched in silence as it sizzled in the fire and slowly began extinguishing the flames.

"What are we going to do now?" Mark asked.

"The cave!" Michelle shouted, looking at Steve. "The one behind the falls. If we can make it there, we can hold them off until morning and then get the hell out of here."

"Chris, how many rounds do you have left?"

"Eleven in this mag and another full mag in my backpack, 28 rounds."

"Make sure they count!" Steve said. "Chris, you lead the way."

Just as Steve said that a huge rock crashed into the

middle of the fire scattering pyramid stacked logs and sending wet coal ash and sizzling embers into a plume. Chris turned the direction the rock seemed to have come from and let loose a three-round volley.

"Move!" Steve shouted.

Chris led the way to the falls as quickly as they could manage in the dark. With only a couple of flashlights, soft earth turning to mud, and scared out of their wits, the trek wasn't easy. Michelle followed Chris, Jennifer was in the middle and Steve, and Mark brought up the rear.

PART 10

Lightning flashed across the valley as booming thunder shook the very ground beneath their feet. Chris saw one of the beasts in the flash of lightning and chanced a couple of rounds. He heard the creature scream, but he didn't know if he hit it or not; he kept running.

They made it to the base of the natural rock staircase that went up and crossed over the falls. The rain was pelting down so hard that they had trouble seeing even with the flashlights. They clambered up the twenty feet to the top to cross over to the other side. Another bolt of lightning crackled, and thunder boomed near them causing Jennifer to stumble. Momentarily blinded, she fell into the water below. Mark made a grab for her and was able to grasp onto her shirt. Steve was at his side in an instant. Together, they hauled the girl out of the water and onto her feet.

"We gotta keep moving," Steve shouted.

BOOM BOOM BOOM

Steve saw the muzzle blasts as his friend opened fire behind them, but he didn't want to look back. They managed to get to their feet and jump across the rock slabs to the other side. Once across, they climbed down the rocks and found the ledge that led behind the falls.

"Turn off the lights, maybe they won't see where we're going now," Steve said.

One by one they slid along the ledge, careful not to slip off the rocks into the crashing water below. Chris felt along the wall until he felt it give way to the interior of the cave.

They crowded together into the opening of the cave and stood huddled together. Jennifer was crying and near hysterics, but Mark was holding her in his arms trying his best to comfort the girl. "We're going to be okay, we're safe now," he soothed.

They stood huddled for several minutes before anyone dared speak.

"Maybe they're gone now. Back to wherever they came from," Chris whispered.

"I don't know, but I'm not leaving this cave until daylight!" Steve replied.

Michelle, listening to the exchange reached a trembling hand out to feel for Steve, "If this st…storm doesn't le…let up, that may be th…the day after to…to…tomorrow."

"Let's move back from the falls, maybe it'll be drier and warmer," Steve suggested.

Chris shuffled back into the cave using Michelle's small flashlight. Keeping the beam small and low on the ground, he found some driftwood that may have floated in at some point. "Maybe we can build a fire and warm up?"

"With what?" Steve asked.

"There's a bit of driftwood here that seems dry, and I have my fire starter kit in my pocket."

"Okay, but let's move further back in so the light isn't seen from outside," Steve whispered.

Chris gathered up the few pieces he could find that lay

near his feet. He didn't want to shine the light all around the cave from fear of being seen from outside. Kneeling, he pulled out his fire-starter kit and went to work.

After several minutes, Steve said "It's not gonna catch dude, might as well give up. Need some kindling."

"Yeah, you're probably right, but it's freezing in here. We need to huddle together and stay warm. We'll wait em out until morning."

Easing down to the hard-rock surface, Steve leaned against the cave wall. Michelle next to him, huddling together. The others joined them, no one speaking, just breathing and trembling.

"What was that?" Michelle whispered.

"What? I didn't hear nothing," Chris said.

"Yeah, me either," Steve said. "We're safe in here. Those things don't know where we are and besides, Chris has the gun. We'll be okay."

Chris leaned back against the cave wall keeping one hand on his pistol. "Hey, let me see that flashlight," he whispered.

He clicked it on, once again, careful with the beam keeping it small and near the ground. "There's a field mouse nest here. We're in business,"

"What's that mean?" Michelle asked.

"It means," Mark said. "He can use it as kindling and get a fire started. Maybe."

Chris pulled the nest apart and laid it in the center of the group. Grabbing the driftwood nearby, he stacked it on top and pulled out his Firestarter kit.

"Cross your fingers."

After a few strikes of the flint, the dry grass caught. It burned rapidly, but Chris and Steve added just a little to it at a time to keep it burning as long as possible.

"Damn, not sure if it'll be enough to get the driftwood

going too."

"Oh my God, it's actually catching. It's going to burn," Michelle said.

The driftwood caught fire in one small area, just a tiny candle sized flame, but it was burning. Soon, the blaze grew larger until a large portion of the driftwood was burning. The small band of hikers scrunched in a circle close to the fire. Michelle saw Steve looking at her. She smiled

"I'm starving," Mark said.

"I can't believe how warm it is with such a small fire," Michelle whispered. "What is that smell? It's atrocious."

"It's all of our body heat," Steve replied.

"Can't be that it feels…stuffy," Chris said. He switched on the flashlight. He never fired another shot.

Jennifer's scream was ripped from her throat.

9. HALLOW FOREST

By AARIKA COPELAND

Every forest had magic. Each one brimmed with wonder and awe.

Some forests had fairies, their twinkling lights helping to guide travelers safely through. Other forests had older magic, the kind that only came from nature itself, lush greenery that homed thousands of creatures working as one.

This was not one of those forests.

Darkness burrowed into the heart of Hallow Forest. Bare limbs of trees stretched outward like bony fingers to ward off wandering travelers. Locals feared this place. They feared the things that scurried underfoot, and of the eyes that seemed to watch from the darkness. An unknown world lurked within, a quiet one eager to come alive.

Tonight, it would breathe again. Tonight, it was Halloween.

***

HALLOW FOREST

Elizabeth Applegate brought up the rear of the group. Weighted by the pack on her back and a magician's cape that hung a tad too long - she still needed another foot to fill it out completely – she struggled to keep up.

"Come on!" Susie called from the top of the hill. "She can't keep up. We shouldn't have brought her."

Elizabeth bid her legs to go faster, but in her haste she stumbled over the cloak, sending her to the ground on her hands and knees. The magician tools in her pack thudded against her spine as she fell, forcing a hiss from her lips.

A collective sigh rose from the rest of the group, a sound that prodded Elizabeth like accusatory fingers.

"She should just go home!" One shouted.

"We are going to miss out on all the good houses if we have to wait around for her all night," another called.

"Stop it." Jordan was by Elizabeth's side, reaching down to help her to her feet.

Elizabeth swatted away Jordan's hand, perfectly capable of standing on her own.

Elizabeth and Jordan had met five years ago, in a kindergarten class, and were close for a time. Once Elizabeth's mother fell ill, Jordan was the only person who concerned herself with Elizabeth's mother's well-being. Not even Elizabeth's grandmother could take time away from her nightly gambles to query about her daughter's health, much less her granddaughter's. But as both Elizabeth's mother and time passed, Elizabeth drew away from Jordan.

But that Halloween night, as Jordan and the others had gone away from their town's annual haunted maze, where most children volunteered for a chance to scare their parents, she had noticed Elizabeth performing one of her magic acts along the ticket lines. Jordan offered Elizabeth an invitation to tag along for a night of trick-or-treating. It was easy for Elizabeth to distract herself with a festive flare, mask the broken girl beneath the cape. But at that moment, Elizabeth had taken a chance and said yes.

Grinding metal sounded in Elizabeth's ears, tugging her back to the moment, reminding her of the group's self-proclaimed leader. Susie. Susie was the only one other than Elizabeth not dressed to scare, and she stretched to her full height at the sound of hissing, splintered wood, her round belly protruding from underneath the top of her two-piece, tutu princess dress.

Susie's father was the lead man on the new property development east of town, the one digging through Hallow Forest at all times of the day and night. The new girl with a piggy bank, Susie was favorited no matter how malicious her attitude. "I am not missing out on the big-sized Butterfingers," Susie said. A few others echoed their concerns too. Their complaints quieted when the sound of crunching leaves came from their right, just inside the border of Hallow Forest. It moved fast, retreating only to scurry forward again. Elizabeth's pack clamored against her back as she scrambled into a sprint toward the security of the group.

"It's Hallow Forest," Jordan whispered once she joined Elizabeth and the others in a tight circle, their eyes trained to the woods in front of them. "It's haunted. No one ever goes in, and nothing ever comes out. I don't even think animals live in there."

They all knew the stories. The unearthly noises that emanated from beyond the trees. Sightings of ghosts proclaimed by those foolish enough to venture too deep. The trees themselves fueled the myths, their trunks and limbs barren and dead year-round, spindly branches

HALLOW FOREST

reaching outward, challenging the curiosities of the townsfolk.

"Then what was that sound?" Elizabeth piped. "If nothing lives in there, what made that sound?"

"Why don't you go find out," Susie added. A chuckle came from the rest of the kids, acting as an invitation for Susie to continue. "Elizabeth, if you want to trick or treat with us, prove you are worth waiting around for. Go check out what that noise was."

Elizabeth felt their wicked smiles at the dare. She trained her feet in the direction of Hallow Forest, unwilling to let them see the horror now splayed across her features. Why had she accepted Jordan's invitation? She knew better than to think she would be welcome unconditionally. Was it even a surprise that she was singled out? No. But she repelled the idea of admitting her distress. So, she stepped closer to the woods. The scurrying sounded again, and the children behind her howled with a mixture of fright and excitement.

"Come on, don't be chicken!" someone shouted. "Move closer."

Elizabeth pressed closer to the tree line, a quiet moan escaping her lips. They stood on the crest of a hill where the sun shone the last of its rays, the land around them still cast in full autumn colors of orange and red. But with each step, the world grew darker, the trees grew higher. Cold sweat dampened her temples as she came to a stop at the edge of Hallow Forest and peered through the weaving trunks.

"I don't see anything," Elizabeth said, looking back over her shoulder.

"You need to get closer," Susie's words were as sharp as the sneer on her face. "Bet you can't spend three minutes in there without running back crying."

Elizabeth faced the woods again, fighting the excessive thumping in her chest. The wind hissed through the empty woods, a whisper of sorts that compelled her to listen carefully.

"Wait." Jordan's voice banished the whispers Elizabeth had been entranced by, and Elizabeth was thankful for the interruption. "You don't have to do this. We don't know what's out there."

Elizabeth narrowed her eyes at Jordan. Hadn't Jordan suspected the fine print of her invitation might contain such conditions?

Jordan noted the look in Elizabeth's eyes and looked away. Jordan unclasped the watch on her wrist and fiddled with a few buttons. She held it out to Elizabeth at first but took Elizabeth's right hand in her own when Elizabeth refused it. Jordan strapped the watch to Elizabeth's wrist. "I set the timer. Show them you're no chicken."

Elizabeth nodded and swallowed. She peeled off her pack, raised her flashlight, and took a step past the tree line.

She breathed in the earthy tones of the forest, the damp earth and moss mingled with the hint of decay. A breeze blew, moaning as it slid around the trees. Elizabeth pulled the magician's cape tight around her, glancing down at the neon glow of the watch.

Three minutes was all she needed to endure to prove herself. Many things can happen in three minutes. The thought squeezed its way into her mind and sent a prickle across her scalp. She tried not to think about how quickly her mother had slipped away in her final moments.

A pale orange hue hung near the ground in the distance, the last remnants of a day past, and Elizabeth was thankful for the flashlight in her hand. The tops of the trees were twisted above her, spreading out like spider webs waiting to capture unsuspecting prey. The moist earth and rotted leaves beneath her sucked at her feet. Elizabeth found this odd. She had never known any tree in Hallow Forest to bare leaves. The concern was fleeting as she again looked at the iridescent glow of the watch. 2:18 and counting down.

A scratching sound, like squirrels running in the trees, stole her attention. She shined the light to the barren canopies above, and as the beam cut across the treetops, she caught the shape of something. She could not make out the figure entirely because it promptly scurried up a tree trunk and out of sight.

Turning, Elizabeth tried to see back to Jordan and the others. But she was met with a dense wall of saplings. The hilltop was gone. Had she wondered that far away? She had hardly moved. Hadn't she?

"Guys? Are you out there?" The darkness swallowed her whispered words. Her throat worked as she slid her free hand over the side of her pants, thinking that she may have just alerted whatever supernatural creatures lived within Hallow Forest to her presence?

As if in answer to her thoughts, the scurrying sounded from behind her, running a tingle down her back. She retreated deeper into the cape, imagining the draped fabric were her mother's protective arms.

Elizabeth's mother had owned a magic and costume shop in town, and Elizabeth had often helped sort through new merchandise, playing dress up and modeling the costumes, striking silly poses until her mother barked with laughter.

One day, Elizabeth's mother had wanted to clear out an old storage room, and as Elizabeth sifted through moth-eaten boxes and raggedy pre-used costumes, she came upon a trunk, it's surface embossed in silver filigree. She unhitched the latches, and its mouth yawned with a loud creak as she eased the lid open. Inside, Elizabeth found a perfectly folded cape, silver threaded stars stitched across a sky of shifting purples and deep blues. The colors layered one another but never seemed to mix: oil against water, threads of stardust and divinity.

Elizabeth had presented the cape to her mother, saying, "You have to play the part."

Her mother's expression was reminiscent when she locked eyes on the cape in Elizabeth's hands, and it lit her whole face. Her mother laughed and pulled it over her shoulders, asking how it fared against the copper red of her hair. "It's been a long time since I last wore this."

"You've seen it before."

"Yes." Her mother's eyes soaked in the midnight colors, glistening with untold stories.

"Where did it come from? It looks like it is made with magic."

"Oh, yes. It is indeed." Her mother's eyes met Elizabeth's. "But magic comes in many forms, my love. Trust. Kindness. Forgiveness. These are a few. You must unlock the rest for yourself."

Elizabeth had believed her. Her mother glowed with her own kind of magic that Elizabeth doubted she could ever match.

But in the end, it wasn't enough to save her. And now Elizabeth had only the cape to remind her of her mother's warmth.

Scratching came from above, and Elizabeth forced her feet to move in tandem with the sound, following it with the beam of her light. Whatever it was, it jumped from tree to tree, until eventually stopping on the tree directly in front of her.

Her body went rigid, and she blinked several times as she stared at the creature caught within the beam of her flashlight. A creature in semblance to an oversized mountain toad, but not quite. Swaying at his back like a pendulum was a long tail. Pokey ears jutted out by large, round yellow eyes that reflected the glow of Elizabeth's flashlight with all the eeriness of a nocturnal creature. The fangs protruding from his upper gums grew unevenly, forcing one side of his lower lip to hang further down than the other, giving the beast what looked like a permanent half frown. He grasped the trunk with sharp talons and seemed to inspect Elizabeth just as much as she was he.

"What are you?" Elizabeth's words were no louder than a mouse's squeak.

He scurried around the tree, tilting his head as he took her in at different angles.

Elizabeth cleared her throat and tried again. "H-Hello."

The creature stopped when she spoke. Elizabeth and the creature were now eye level. But she was not afraid. On the contrary, apprehension untethered its hold on her as she stared into his molten gold eyes.

"Do you know where my friends are?"

The creature shook his head so fast spit flung in every direction, drenching Elizabeth's costume. She backed away, holding her arms out to see slobber dripping off the cloak.

A beep escaped the watch on her wrist then, and Elizabeth quickly pushed the button on the side of the clock to silence the timer. The three minutes were finished, but how was she to know which direction back to the hilltop? Trees rose above her as far as she could see.

A weight hit her shoulder, and she stiffened under the sudden abnormal weight. Craning her neck, Elizabeth saw that the creature had jumped from the tree to her shoulder, where he now settled on his haunches, blinking one eye at a time, his low hanging lip dripping more drool.

He smelled of stagnant water, of cold breeze and the

faint scent of rotten wood. Blue warts sporadically rose over his otherwise smooth, moss green skin. There was no way this was just some toad. He was something special.

"Umm," Elizabeth stammered "I'm Elizabeth Applegate."

He responded in a series of croaks and chirps, sounding something like scruh, scruh, scruhm.

"Hi, Scrum."

Scrum shifted his gaze down the cape, running his four-fingered hand across the delicate fabric.

"Do you know the way out, Scrum?"

Scrum looked up, the corners of his lips turning up over his fangs. He grunted and pointed his taloned finger.

"That's the way out?"

Scrum clicked his tongue against his fangs, continuing to hold out his finger. To Elizabeth, all the trees appeared the same. She wasn't sure if trusting Scrum was the best solution, but it was her only one. She could wander around aimlessly and hope to locate the way out, but how long would that take? Hoping she would not come to regret her decision, Elizabeth took off in the direction of Scrum's pointed finger.

As they walked, Elizabeth tried convincing Scrum to quiet his spat of garbled grunts and chirps, told him that these woods were haunted, dangerous even. Scrum paid no mind, seemingly oblivious to the communication barrier between them. No apparitions appeared though. No beasts howled at the moon, unless Elizabeth counted the construction machines in the distance. In fact, the woods were void of most earthly sounds, save for Scrum's squawking's, and the crunch of dried leaves and snapped twigs from beneath Elizabeth's shoes. Maybe Hallow Forest was not the place she had believed it was.

Soon, Elizabeth confided in Scrum her daily life. "Most

days the magician act is well received," she said. She explained how this small accomplishment made her believe she would not need to hide behind those tricks forever. "One day, I'll retire the cape. Mom always said there was more to magic than a cape and a handful of tricks." But inwardly, she feared the day the cape was no longer needed.

Scrum listened but made no indication of understanding anything Elizabeth said. And nor did Elizabeth care. For the first time since her mother died, she had a listening ear. She wouldn't speak of her mother's passing to Scrum though. That path was darker than the one they walked now.

After about an hour of walking, and after Elizabeth had poured out all her thoughts and feelings, a new realization dawned. Surely by now, they were near the opposite end of Hallow Forest, but the trees continued to extend before her into an indecipherable labyrinth.

Elizabeth halted, taking in the shape of the moon and where it hung in the sky. On aching and wobbling legs, she turned around. No way could she traverse back through without Scrum's help. Could they have gone in circles? She felt the limbs of the trees press in on her, the unworldly silence of the forest wrapped her in a cocoon, and her temples began a slow rhythm of whomp, whomp, whomp.

Her stomach rumbled its displeasure, reminding her she had skipped her frozen waffle dinner in her haste to perform her new act at the entrance of the haunted maze.

Elizabeth's feet stumbled and crossed, and she caught herself against a tree.

"Scrum," she half pleaded, "this isn't right. Where are you taking me? Please, I can't stay out here. I'm cold and I'm hungry."

Scrum hopped onto the tree above Elizabeth and vanished in a scurry. Elizabeth's breathing hitched, and she slid her hands over her face, feeling her chin quiver beneath. She may never get out of Hallow Forest if she continued to follow directions from a little monster. What was she thinking? Was she so deprived of companionship that she imagined Scrum to be more than the animal he was? It was well past dark, the wind had picked up, blowing her cape in a swirl around her legs, and the sound of the construction workers on the other side of town made her shiver whenever the whining of the engines broke through the silence of the woods.

Her heart fluttered against her chest at that thought. Perhaps she could follow those sounds. Find a way out of this mess! But the emptiness of Hallow Forest caused the noises to echo around her, making it impossible to register which direction the construction site might be.

She sank to the ground, her heart following, and she curled herself against the crook of the tree trunk. If she sat there long enough maybe the tree would eventually overtake her body. She could finally belong somewhere. She studied her hands as they lay listless on the ground, curious about how long the process might take.

Elizabeth made it to the count of seventy-three when her body stilled at the sudden reappearance of Scrum who sat on his haunches, a toppling amount of gray, leaking, and rotting vegetation in his hands. She let out a heavy breath, relieved to see his face, but when her lungs expanded again, they brought in a sickly sweet scent. "Ugh." She backed away from his offering.

Scrum lifted a half-rotted fruit to his mouth, shoving it in and chewed messily. Elizabeth turned her face away, embarrassed by the gooey bits dripping from his mouth. Scrum scrambled up the tree, angling himself to her and grumbling. He pawed at her shoulder. When she turned to face him again, she was taken aback to see the fruit in his hand slowly beginning to reverse its rot. Soft spots hardened, its flesh repaired. A ripe, red apple once more. Her eyes grew wide, and her stomach gnawed.

She didn't think about how Scrum made the apple possible. Did not care if it were some trick to get her to eat the fruit. Elizabeth took the apple and sank her teeth into its flesh, juices running down the sides of her mouth.

When Elizabeth finished her third apple, her stomach no longer wailed like a banshee. She thanked Scrum while licking the last of the sticky substance from her fingers. Scrum clicked his talons happily. He found his perch on her shoulder and urged her again into the direction they had previously traveled.

Elizabeth hauled herself up off the ground, feeling replenished and healthy, and continued their trek through the forest, her faith in the little creature restored.

Soon, they came upon a tree that seemed to scratch the surface of the stars. The thick trunk twisted from its base to the branches like a tightly wound spring ready to pounce. Luminescent tendrils of moss swayed in the breeze from the canopy. Roots jutted from the ground around its base, an unfurling of lucent green moss over their surface, and surrounded the tree like a wooden moat.

Scrum pointed toward the tree and Elizabeth's heart split. What a wonder she beheld. And how cold and stiff her limbs felt.

"No. I need out of here, Scrum. Please. Take me home!"

Scrum growled and scurried down the loose fabric of her magician's cape, stopping at her feet and bunching a handful of her robe between his talons, trying to draw her forward. Elizabeth planted her feet and crossed her arms, frowning down at him.

"I'll find my own way then."

Scrum let go then and hopped around, stomping his feet and whipping his tail. He stopped and lifted his head to the sky, bellowing out another bought of scruhm sounds.

A dull buzzing grew in the distance, gradually becoming stronger. Elizabeth held up her flashlight, shining its yellow light to the treetops when a she felt a small pressure hit her hand. She lowered the torch to her hand to inspect. A small black bug crawled over her knuckles and in between her fingers.

"Ouch! It bit me."

She swatted away the insect. Another quickly took its place. Dozens of the insects now buzzed around her, zipping past her ears and face. The air above her seemed to vibrate and she looked up with the flashlight to see a legion of them blotting out the glow of the moon. The mass formed an angle downward and sped through the air.

Elizabeth staggered, swatting at the bugs now nipping her skin. She bunched the extra length of her robe in her hands and ran. There was nowhere to hide. She surveyed the ground for Scrum, but he had disappeared again.

"Scrum! Where are you?"

She trampled her way toward the old tree, rounding broken branches and leaping over raised roots. She caught sight of Scrum on the trunk of the twisted tree ahead. He pointed down to an opening in the chest of the tree. A hollow. Elizabeth ran, twigs whipping at her face as she flew through the space between her and the opportunity of cover. More than once, her cape entangled on the roots that suddenly began to rise and fall around her like ocean currents. But she did not have time to wonder how or why they moved; it was not as important as getting away from those biting insects.

She plummeted to the ground when her foot caught beneath one of the roots as it submerged back beneath the earth. The flashlight cracked and faltered as it connected to the trunk as she fell.

The pounding in her skull pulverized her thoughts. She was stuck. She could not see. Her lungs worked over time. The sound of writhing insect wings came fast, flanked by the creaking bend of wood. She clawed at the ground around her encased sneaker, keenly aware of the mud burrowing underneath her fingernails.

The thought of those insects crawling over her face and sweeping through her hair turned her blood to ice. Her foot wiggled, her hands forming deep cavities around her ankle.

The first bug landed on her face, and she wiped it away, smearing mud across her cheek. The second buzzed near her ear, and she lifted her shoulder to knock it away. Her hands trembled, and her foot was no closer to release.

Just then, Elizabeth felt something tunnel against the bottom of her trapped shoe. It wiggled against her, pushing on the sole. Her foot was set free, and she jumped up, ignoring the ache in her ankle. She sprinted the rest of the way, avoiding the few roots left in her path. Elizabeth swore she could feel the hint of a breeze from the beat of hundreds of combined wings. She dove into the hollow, rolling onto her back. Dragging herself backward on her elbows, she faced the hoard of bugs now so close the buzz seemed to come from inside her skull.

Surprise squealed out of her lips when Scrum's head popped up between her legs from beneath a layer of leaves. Scrum faced the opening of the hollow where the swarm was only inches from entering. He let out a howl, and the bugs slowed, coming to a stop and hovering in a body just outside the opening like a dark curtain.

Elizabeth sighed. Safety was a relative term, and she was not sure it applied to this moment. But Scrum somehow knew they would remain unharmed inside the hollow. Is that why he led her here? Had he known the insects would come for her?

"My foot. Did you do that?"

Scrum turned to her, again blinking one eye at a time, his tongue sitting on his bottom lip. Elizabeth took this as a yes.

"What are those things?" Elizabeth asked, more to herself than him, knowing he would not provide any logical answer.

Scrum suddenly sunk beneath the dried leaves and Elizabeth could hear him rummage around her ankles. He moved like a shark beneath gray waters, popping up again somewhere behind her, deeper into the hollow. She had not noticed just how deep the hollow seemed to go. He beckoned for her to follow. Elizabeth chanced another glance at the opening, tiring of the waiting game she found herself playing with Scrum. But the path outside was blocked by the buzzing insects, and he had saved her multiple times now. There was not a straight path back to where she began, but she believed Scrum would keep her safe, as he had done so far on their journey together. She hauled herself up and followed.

The hollow wove from right to left, down then up, and broke into several other passages. Elizabeth stayed close, her ankle aching with every step. The flashlight she had managed to hold onto through the fall hindered, and she continuously rapped it against her leg to keep it illuminated.

After several turns, voices echoed along the roots that formed the tunnels. She felt a swell of hope in her chest.

"There are people down here? Someone will know how to get me home!"

Elizabeth hobbled along faster now, ignoring her foot's protest. Scrum led her toward a grand opening at the end of the tunnel. She stopped short of entering the chamber. The air emanating from the room made the hairs on her arms stand on end. The scent was metallic and thick, like an early morning thunderstorm. She spied a massive cauldron taking up the bulk of the space in the room. It sat atop a blazing fire that gave off no warmth, but a cooling sensation that hit Elizabeth's face and bled into her very being. Purple smoke bubbled over the lip of the kettle, crackling and sparking as if electrified, then continued to cascade to the ground, slithering across the floor before disappearing into a haze.

Mesmerized by what she saw, Elizabeth's feet pulled her forward into the room.

Standing on two stacked toadstools, stirring the contents of the cauldron, hunched a young girl, perhaps Elizabeth's age. Goggles emphasized her already frizzy hair that poked out in every direction from beneath a brimmed witch's hat. The girl wore a cinched black dress and black shoes that came to a long-curled point past her toes.

The girl did not notice Elizabeth or Scrum's entrance and was busily talking to someone Elizabeth could not yet see.

"Yes, yes. I added frog's toe. And don't even think about asking if I put the poison berry in!" she said, pointing the spoon in her hand accusingly to whomever she spoke. She placed the spoon back in the pot, peering down into the substance, her mouth pinched to one side.

"I am only here to help," her companion answered.

Elizabeth's eyes widened. A living skeleton came into view. He stretched near the height of the tree they stood within, long black pants covered his skeletal legs, and he wore a long-sleeved black dress jacket dusted with cobwebs and embellished with dangling spiders.

The skeleton peered through thick rounded spectacles

that remained in place despite his lack of nose. With empty eyes, he stared down at an open book sitting on top of a cobwebbed easel. He ran his bony fingertips across the page, occasionally tapping before lifting his top hat and scratching the curve of his skull underneath.

The girl stirring the cauldron hopped off the enormous toadstools and moved toward a table in the opposite corner. She grabbed a handful of something and jumped back up to toss it in the brew. The smoke crackled with sparks before turning into a summer sunset shade and shifting the scent of the room into something sweet and crisp, like the effervescent of a peeled orange. Warmth replaced the previous coolness of the fire and hit Elizabeth full force in the face.

"There," she said. "That seems better, but still not right. No one has awoken. What will we do! Midnight nears. And this tonic is not working."

Just then, a movement in the corner caught Elizabeth's eye. A white sheet billowed in a phantom breeze. No! It was hovering on its own, moving toward her, staring at her through sunken holes in the fabric. A small stub stuck out from the body, waving at her with great enthusiasm. The corners of the sheet where she suspected the mouth to be, turned up into something like a smile. A ghost? Yes!

Elizabeth stared at a real ghost.

Scrum ran ahead and was now in the center of the hollow. He waved his hands in the air, trying to gain everyone's attention. He jumped up and down, snapping his fangs, but the skeleton and the girl paid no mind to him. Not until Scrum started growling and snarling, clicking his talons together as he continued to jump maniacally.

The girl still argued, insistent on having the last word, but the skeleton turned his head and stared at Elizabeth. His jaw dropped low, it unhinged and fell straight into the cauldron.

"You sorry sack of bones, you've ruined it now! And what in the hairy toadstools are you staring at?"

The girl followed the skeleton's empty gaze to Elizabeth. She jumped and hovered in place, clicking her black heels together before drifting back down. Elizabeth shook her head at the sight, sure that her eyes deceived her. The girl hopped down from the stools and rushed past the eagerly jumping Scrum, straight to Elizabeth. She grabbed Elizabeth's hands and spun her around once, then pulled her into a tight hug.

"Finally!" she exclaimed. "It has worked. Sir Skeleton, they are waking."

Elizabeth stiffened under the girl's grip. She thought about running, eyeing the archway and the tunnel beyond. She did not care if those bugs blocked the exit. She would run straight through them. Run until she found the border.

But she could not. The opening was quickly overgrown by the underground root system, trapping them all inside the hollow.

The girl released Elizabeth and kneeled to Scrum.

Sir Skeleton fished his jaw out of the cauldron and reattached it as he moved forward. "Wherever did you find her?" he asked.

Scrum made his usual scrappy sounds, but Sir Skeleton and the girl seemed to understand, nodding along while listening. They gasped before focusing on Elizabeth. The girl asked, "you woke near the edge?" "The edge?" Elizabeth mimed, too shocked to conjure any other question.

"You should not have woken so close," answered Sir Skeleton. "Something is amiss, dear Franny," he said to the girl with the frazzled hair who had pulled her goggles down to hang around her neck, revealing deep imprints encompassing her eyes from where they once sat.

Elizabeth mustered the courage to answer. "I was-wasn't sleeping. I was trick-or-treating, with my friends."

"Trick-or-treat?" Franny jumped back, her feet taking a moment to touch the ground again. "Scrum! She is no witch. She's just a girl in costume."

Scrum seemed to be arguing, snapping his fangs and shaking his head, spit flinging in all directions. Franny listened, and her face gradually fell from shock to something else. She eyed Elizabeth from behind her extra-long fluttering lashes.

"What is he saying?" Elizabeth demanded.

"He says, you are indeed the witch we need," answered Sir Skeleton as he hunkered over, his brow bones turning up like eyebrows as he stared at Elizabeth.

The ghost came closer, hiding behind Franny's leg but continued to wave at Elizabeth.

"No. I'm Elizabeth. Just a girl. No witch. I need to get back to my friends."

Franny folded her arms across her chest. "Take her to the border, Scrum. We have work to do." Franny turned from Elizabeth and hopped back up to her perch above the cauldron.

Sir Skeleton stood and moved on his stilt legs back to the easel, again scanning his boney fingers along the pages.

Scrum gave up, his lip hanging low and his arms hanging lower. Just then, a great rumbling reached deep inside the hollow, reverberating across the roots and sounding like a howling beast. In a moment, the shy ghost was by Elizabeth's side, clinging to her leg with his nubs.

Elizabeth gave the ghost a weary smile. "Don't worry." She scooted away from him. "It is only the construction site. You know, machines."

"What did you say?" Sir Skeleton asked.

"The sound, it's a tractor. Susie's dad runs the construction site at the edge of town."

"Do you hear that, Franny?"

Franny's mouth formed an 'o,' but she regained her composure by crossing her arms and turning her nose up and away.

Sir Skeleton continued. "Perhaps, our dear Scrum Mosswater is correct, and this girl is indeed the witch we need."

"Please. I said before I am no witch. I'm just a trickster, sleight of hand, misdirection, a cheap magician. I don't know real magic."

"There are many forms of magic. Maybe, you have yet to realize your own. We need your help, Miss Elizabeth. Will you help these forgotten souls?"

Elizabeth's body laxed beneath the weight of her situation. Heat from the cauldron enveloped her. It was too hot in here. Sweat gathered at the base of her neck and trickled down her back. She fumbled to form her thoughts, each one slipping from her grasp and rolling away. She knew they all watched, waited as she ran a hand through her hair. "What is it you need?"

Sir Skeleton gave a slight nod before speaking. "The roots of this tree"—Sir Skeleton expanded his long arms, gesturing to the room in which they stood— "stretches all through Hallow Forest. The sap is powerful magic. It allows us to slumber year round and wake but once a year. Our tree is what keeps us safe from the outside world."

Scrum grunted and kicked his taloned toes at Sir Skeleton.

"Of course, other than our trusted guardian, Scrum Mosswater, who creates the necessary mischief to deter humans from coming too close," Sir Skeleton added, appeasing Scrum.

Elizabeth squinted down at Scrum. "Necessary mischief?" Realization hit her. "The bugs…?" She said accusingly.

Scrum dug the talons of his toes into the dirt, avoiding her gaze.

Sir Skeleton continued before Elizabeth could dwell on the matter too long.

"The tree is damaged, Elizabeth. We did not know how or why. But you do. These machines, as you call them. We must heal the severed roots, or the magic will not flow. No one else will wake, and we will fade to dust at midnight. We cannot leave the parameters of the forest and it is dangerous to allow the outside world to see us. It would be too dangerous. And nothing we do is of use if these machines continue to dig up our home."

Just then, the hollow shook, vibrations running up and down the wooden innings.

"Enough blabbering! If we don't hurry, the whole forest will be destroyed, and us along with it. What is your plan?" Franny demanded.

They all looked at her again, which turned her throat dry. What was she to say? People in town hardly listened to Elizabeth as it was, an orphan girl with who wandered through the streets performing her ticks. How would they respond if she were to ask them to stop digging?

"I don't, uhh, I mean…" Her words scratched at her throat as she tried to force them out. Elizabeth couldn't meet their gaze.

This was all too much. What did they expect from her? Her worth was measured through whispers and stares she received. Her heart clenched at that thought.

"She does not wish to help us, Sir Skeleton." The small amount of hope Elizabeth spied in Franny's face now melted into disappointment as she spoke. "Elizabeth wishes to be back with her friends, and we are no such thing to her."

At that, Scrum sounded a series of croaks, and Sir Skeleton's head tilted a bit.

"What did he say?" Elizabeth asked.

It was Franny who answered. "Scrum says you have no friends. That they abandoned you."

But that was not true. Her friends waited for her on the hill. The moment her mind conjured the thought she knew how untrue it was. Elizabeth had slowed their group. Wasn't it why she was dared to enter Hallow Forest? Those three minutes passed long ago. Would they still be waiting? No. But these creatures were. They had been waiting for someone just like her. And now they waited for her response, very much wanting and needing her to be here.

Elizabeth did not know if even Jordan was a faithful friend. But the skeleton, the witch, the small ghost, and the hopping amphibian at her feet indeed had friends, and they were desperately trying to get back to them. What could she do though? Merely asking the workers to stop was no use. And her bag of magic props was left on the hill.

"Yes, well." Sir Skeleton's neck joints rattled as if he were clearing his throat. "It was delightful meeting you, Elizabeth Applegate. Scrum, might you please escort our trickster back to the border."

That was it. Trickster. Elizabeth never needed much to fool her audiences into believing whatever she chose to show them. Just a flavor, enough to distract their attention from the truth masked beneath the deception.

"Wait!" Elizabeth exclaimed. "I have an idea."

Elizabeth beamed at each of them before landing on Scrum. He licked his fangs, his mouth forming what she believed was likely a smile.

Scrum had believed in her since the very beginning, had chosen her. Even with unsavory methods of asking for help. Looking down at him, Elizabeth saw herself the way Scrum did. Someone worthy of trust and courage, but she did not fail to see the creature who had risked so much by believing in her. Her pulse thrummed with excitement, and she smiled back at his toothy grin.

***

Outside, the night hung heavy. The flashlight flickered and died a few yards from the tree's base. The roots lied on the ground like slumbering beasts, and Elizabeth tread carefully over their arched backs even though she suspected Franny's presence cast them into their petrified state.

Elizabeth's movements were stiff, her ankle begging for rest. Franny took notice. She removed a vial from the pouch tied about her waist, kneeled, then raised the hem of Elizabeth's pants. The flesh underneath was shiny and red with swelling. Franny opened the vial and wrapped her soft fingers around Elizabeth's ankle, angling it so she could drip two silver drops of liquid. She lowered Elizabeth's foot to the ground. "That should be better."

At first, it itched, but soon a cooling sensation took over and the pressure released. Good as new after a few seconds.

"Thank you," Elizabeth said.

"Hmm," Franny answered with a shrug while pocketing the vial. For a moment, a fracture formed in Franny's austere character: a fissure along the combative walls surrounding her that allowed for a glimpse to the compassionate witch beneath. Her next words repaired that crack. "Humans are such brittle things. Easily succumbed to the right amount of pressure."

HALLOW FOREST

"Franny, take care. Were we not the same, once? Succumbed by a great loss?" Sir Skeleton said, and Elizabeth wondered briefly what great loss they had endured.

Franny pinched her mouth and took Ghost's nub in her child-sized hand.

"Scrum, would you mind?" Sir Skeleton said.

Scrum howled. Hundreds of fireflies descended a moment later, swirling around Scrum like a golden tornado of stars, and Scrum took pleasure in chasing them. Franny *actually* giggled when Ghost pulled his nub from her hand and wove through the bugs alongside Scrum. The bugs spun through the air like a school of fish and realigned. Scrum sounded another command and the bugs scattered, lighting a path in front of them like a regal glowing carpet.

"Ah, that is better," Sir Skeleton said.

Ghost floated into position next to Franny, Sir Skeleton sauntered to the rear, and Elizabeth followed behind Scrum as he led them along the strip of bobbing lights that cut through Hallow Forest's dark frontier.

***

As the five of them moved closer to uncertain peril, Elizabeth found solace from the woods around her. She strained her senses to take it all in. Where silence once blanketed Hallow Forest, crickets now chirped. The flapping of leathery wings brought silhouettes shooting across the light of the moon. Spiders crocheted their webs into large, elaborate patterns between branches, gleaming with midnight dew. Elizabeth drank it all in and wondered how anyone could overlook such beauty.

A light cut across her vision. Unnatural against her surroundings. Laughter chased the erratic movement of light. Between a thicket of saplings to her right, Elizabeth spotted Jordan. She had not realized how close to town they had come. Jordan sat in the grass on a hill. Her shoulders curled inward, as she stared intently at the ground. The other children from the trick-or-treat party laughed around her as they shined their flashlights down into their buckets and sacks of candy. They were here! An urge to burst through the foliage and claim she'd survived Hallow Forest, to see their faces as they stared at the conquering hero, surged within her.

A beam of light lit Elizabeth's face as she nursed the thought.

"Elizabeth?" someone called. "Is that you?"

Startled, Elizabeth looked back to her band of fantastical misfits, but they, along with the fireflies, had vanished. She turned in a circle, but all trace of them diffused into the night.

Elizabeth turned back to see the children, the light still pinned on her face. The faces of many children now peered back at her through the brush. Elizabeth followed the light and came through the brush. As she walked out onto the hill, somewhere in the distance, the sound of splitting wood could be heard.

"Elizabeth, it is you!"

Jordan was on her feet now and rushed Elizabeth. The rest of the group followed close behind, their flashlights all finding Elizabeth's face.

"We searched for you. We thought you were lost for good!"

Jordan was by her side, eyes wide, taking in Elizabeth's dirty face and cape. "What happened to you?" she gasped.

Before Elizabeth could answer, someone else spoke. "She looked for you."

A part formed in the center of the group to allow Susie

to step through. The lights fell away from Elizabeth's face and focused on Susie. "We thought you were chicken and took off instead of fessing up to being a wimp."

Susie approached.

"Have you been in Hallow Forest this whole time?" Jordan's pinched face was as incredulous as the question.

"I found something!" Elizabeth confessed.

"Now we know you're a liar," Susie spat. "There isn't anything in Hallow Forest."

"No. The stories are true. There are ghosts."

Dread and guilt broiled in the pit of her stomach. She had just revealed the secret, the truth that Sir Skeleton and the others entrusted her with. She could not stop now. She had to explain.

"I mean, he isn't scary like everyone says. He is kinda shy, the ghost. Witches live in there too. The one I met goes by Franny. She's a bit cranky. And skeletons. Walking, talking skeletons! They said they need my help." Her words were a torrent she did not know how to slow.

Silence extended through the group. Jordan stared, her mouth hanging slightly open. Her eyes shifted in her head as she tried to piece together Elizabeth's sudden outburst.

Susie laughed a deep, belly shaking laugh that doubled as a decree for the others to follow. The children nervously obeyed.

"You are crazy, huh? Ghosts? Witches? Talking skeletons? You should be locked in a looney bin!" Susie spat out between chuckles.

Elizabeth spoke with as much courage and finality as she could muster.

"No, it's true! And your father's construction site is destroying their home."

Susie continued with her taunts. "Applegate, patient 306."

"I'll show you! Just come with me, help me."

"We can help you to the crazy house. Someone, grab her! We'll drag her to the police, tell them she's a ranting loon."

The laughter dwindled and died. No one made a move toward Elizabeth.

Susie didn't wait. She lunged forward. Elizabeth sidestepped out of Susie's reach, quickly searching every face as she did. No one dared meet her eye. No one except Jordan, whose mouth moved indecisively between forming a question and giving an answer.

Elizabeth's eyes pooled with tears, her cheeks burning. Susie regained traction and stalked forward a few steps. Elizabeth did not give her another opportunity. She turned and ran into Hallow Forest, her name trailing her as she sprinted away.

Scrum landed hard on Elizabeth's shoulder. Startled, Elizabeth stumbled in the dark but caught herself as the lightning bugs descended. A tree shifted somewhere ahead, its dim frame lit against the glow of the fireflies. It swept forward only to reveal the thin legs of Sir Skeleton, not a tree at all. Franny and Ghost showed themselves next. Their faces appeared from behind a fallen log.

"Are you alright?" Franny asked. The purple dusting of Franny's cheeks glowed iridescent beneath the light of the fireflies, which heated Elizabeth's cheeks with shame.

Franny should yell, tell her to leave. Not ask over her well-being. Elizabeth had betrayed their secret. And when they turned her away, Elizabeth would indeed be alone. But here she was, asking Elizabeth with more tenderness than she thought capable how she felt.

"I'm sorry. I told them. I shouldn't have done that."

"We saw. We heard," Sir Skeleton answered, which inflamed the heat in her face with the knowledge that they

HALLOW FOREST

witnessed what took place. The charge Susie placed upon her.

Ghost floated to Elizabeth's side and offered the hem of his sheet to wipe away the lone tear that gathered and spilled down her cheek. Ghost's touch was light and airy, crisp, and it doused the flames.

"You betray nothing," Franny said. "Sir Skeleton mentioned the need to keep ourselves concealed, not that you couldn't speak of us to others. It was a bit thoughtless on your part, but no true harm. To us, that is." Franny's words did not have their usual serration. "You need never apologize for the truth, Elizabeth. There is a power beyond measure in truth."

A small smile toyed at the corners of Franny's lips, but they quickly pinned themselves back into their usual tightness.

Elizabeth nodded in understanding and was immensely grateful for Franny, for them all.

"We must be on our way. Midnight is upon us," Sir Skeleton said.

They all fell back into a pace, and soon they were met with the sound of the machines and the fluorescence of false white light. Their glowing guides took their leave then, snuffing out the light from their bottoms and scattering into the night. Elizabeth and the others inched toward the construction site, taking care to stay in the shadows.

"We all know the plan?" she whispered.

Scrum leaped from her shoulder and made a sound as he landed in the dried leaves. He let out a few growls while running in circles, eager to begin. "Lure them into the woods," Elizabeth said, reiterating the plan. "Distract them without revealing yourselves, and I'll steal the keys to the machines."

They each gave Elizabeth a nod.

"Here." Franny dug into her pouch, producing a star-shaped glass bottle. Inside swirled a metallic shade of green tonic. "The sap of the hollow tree. Only a few drops should restore the roots."

Elizabeth reached for the bottle, her fingers curling around the points of the vial.

"You always have friends in Hallow Forest," Sir Skeleton said.

Ghost moved closer and placed his nub in the crook of Elizabeth's hand.

Gratitude crumbled her ability to speak so she was reduced to giving a gracious nod. Their thanks reaffirmed her, strengthened her spine, and squared her shoulders. Just another trick, she told herself.

Elizabeth left them then and moved to the outer edge of the construction site. Most of the land had been disturbed, trees harvested and stacked in the lot at her left. Unnaturally bright, the floodlights drove away the night and forced her to squint in their presence. Elizabeth took in the number of workers operating the machines and those who meandered around the ground.

A scream rose above the world, echoing into every ear. Franny. That drama queen, Elizabeth thought, smiling. Well done.

The rumble of machines died. Elizabeth spotted several workers exchange glances, not yet entirely convinced to investigate. The treetops on the opposite side of the construction site shook and bent, an undoubtful occurrence of a supernatural force. Another shriek stitched panic and confusion across the faces of the yellow-vested men. Many of them ran into the woods, searching for the source of those screams. Those who chose to stay behind gathered closely to witness the unfolding events.

Elizabeth crept along the banks of disturbed earth

unseen and pulled herself into the nearest machine. Locating the keys, she yanked them out of their slot and pocketed them. She moved to the next device and did the same. The third set of keys refused to loosen. Her sweating palms made the keys slip from her grasp.

A howl came ringing through the air, which trembled Elizabeth's hands as she hastily tried to loosen the keys once more. Something in Scrum's cry lowered a veil of panic, tightening her stomach.

The world dropped out from beneath her as thick arms wrapped around her stomach, yanking her backward and placing her firmly on the ground but not letting go of her arm.

"What do you think you are doing little girl?" a man bellowed from beneath his salt and pepper beard. This man wore black slacks and a fine jacket beneath his orange construction vest.

Elizabeth yanked her arm out of his grasp, and when she did her cloak jingled. The man narrowed his gaze, glancing at the machine behind Elizabeth. He reached a hand into the pocket of her cloak, producing several pairs of keys.

The man's attention deviated from Elizabeth as men came scrambling out of the woods, exchanging wide-eyed glances and a slew of obscenities.

"What's going on?" the man called.

"There's something in those woods. It almost ate me!"

"That's nonsense," the bearded man roared.

"I swear it!"

"What was it?"

"I don't know. I couldn't see it. But it's there. We can't let it get away!"

The bearded man tossed the keys he had retrieved from Elizabeth's pocket back to their respective owners as they ran past. One by one the equipment thundered, motors stuttering and whining to life.

Elizabeth brought trembling hands to her mouth and stumbled away from the scene, suddenly forgotten by the finely dressed man. Her heart hammered in her chest as she watched the machines aim for the exact spot she had left Ghost, Franny, Sir Skeleton and Scrum.

She had failed them. Because of her, the men had a reason to push further, harder, into Hallow Forest. There was little chance of stopping them now.

But she had to try.

A scream squeezed from her throat as she hurried into the path of one of the yellow claw machines, shooting her arms in the air. She refused to budge, even when the wheels were upon her. The driver showed no signs of slowing, no indication that he noticed the girl hopping around on the ground, flailing her arms left and right to attract his attention.

The rich scent of dirt and hot rubber forced its way up her nose. Right before being crushed, an arm snaked out and wrapped around her wrist, jerking her out of harm's way, but not before the velvet cape snagged on the treads, twisting it away from Elizabeth's neck and ripping it to shreds beneath the wheels.

She watched helplessly from the ground where she fell as the metal claws tore away at the trees and roots. Her mother's cape ravaged somewhere among them.

Angry tears welled in her eyes. She forced her gaze away and into the eyes of her rescuer. "You were almost crushed!" Jordan stood over her, enraged.

"It's my fault. I ruined everything. They will never be safe now," Elizabeth confessed, defeat replacing any fear that Jordan was there to steal her away as Susie had earlier suggested.

HALLOW FOREST

Jordan's face softened. "You mean your friends in the forest?"

Failure tightened in Elizabeth's throat. She nodded. Jordan looked up at the construction site and at the machines now plowing a new path through Hallow Forest.

"What can we do?"

Elizabeth sniffled and dug her palms into her eyes, rubbing out the tears.

Out of the shadows behind Jordan, new figures emerged. More of the children from their trick-or-treating group stood behind Jordan. Through masks and face paint, they looked down at Elizabeth with curiosity. "You, you believe me?" Elizabeth squeaked.

Jordan shuffled her feet and looked away. "I don't know. It is a bizarre story. You like magic, and you are good at your tricks." Jordan sucked in a deep breath and darted a quick glance back to Elizabeth. "But I've never known you to lie." She faced Elizabeth now. "And I owe you. I should never have left you alone in Hallow Forest. I should never have let Susie bully you. Can you forgive me?"

Elizabeth peeked around Jordan to the other children, the faces of those she could see dripped with the same silent apologies.

Elizabeth checked the watch on her wrist. 11:37. There was still time. And with their help.... Elizabeth sprung to her feet and hugged Jordan for her willingness to help.

"I forgive you," Elizabeth said, Sir Skeleton's mention of various magic taking flight in her thoughts. She felt light, swept between feelings of laughter, and sweet tasting candies, and comfort.

Elizabeth let go of Jordan and grasped for the vial in her pocket, feeling the points of the star pressing against her palm. She would have to give the workers a grand show, something that would ensure no one would come back to damage Hallow Forest. The machines were powerful, but the magic within the star was equally powerful.

Elizabeth led Jordan and the other children away from the construction site, and when they were far enough, she stopped.

"Scrum! Franny! Sir Skeleton! Ghost!"

Hallow Forest turned into a creaking floorboard as the tips of bare limbs swayed against the wind. Huddled together, the children watched Elizabeth with questioning eyes and furrowed brows.

"Please! It's me, Elizabeth."

Doubt began to slither through the group like a coiling snake, slowly suffocating their belief in Elizabeth. A terrible image bloomed in Elizabeth's mind. Scrum and the others, crushed beneath massive tires. Was she too late?

A scurrying sound leaped from tree to tree. Lights shot across the barren branches as the children endeavored to pin down the sound with their beams.

But the lights soon focused on a thin figure a few yards away. Like a tree coming to life with the popping of gnarled joints. The creature's angular motions forced a combined squeak of concern from the children. No one ran. Instead, they inched closer to Elizabeth.

"Sir Skeleton, thank goodness. Franny, Ghost?"

Scrum's sorrowful moan seeped into the air, into Elizabeth's marrow. Something awful had happened. What, she was not sure. But Franny and Ghost had not made an appearance, and Elizabeth feared the worst.

She could not let it happen to Scrum or Sir Skeleton. She would not.

"Scrum, these are my," Elizabeth hesitated on the next word, observing the group of children cocooned around her. Realizing, underneath their costumes and face paint, they were just as frightened as she had been, just as exposed. Elizabeth had the opportunity to help them understand. "Friends," she finished. "They are my friends. They want to help."

Scrum chirped, and the clatter of what could only be Sir Skeleton's applause.

"This time, don't be shy."

If they were to pull this off, they would need to show the workers the truth, albeit sprinkled with a bit of misdirection. That's where Jordan and the others came in.

She pulled out the star-shaped vial and thrust it into the air, the liquid glowing like the north star. If it were green, that is.

"Whoa!" Jordan and the others stared at the mystical substance, no doubt that Elizabeth held the makings of real magic.

"What do we do?" Jordan asked, awestruck.

Elizabeth looked out to the various monstrous creatures and costumes before her. "Everyone remembers their parts from the haunted maze?"

Mischievous smiles and quick nods met her question.

***

Back at the border of the construction site, Elizabeth's friends moved into their positions. Jordan directed them to a ready version of their haunted maze routine. The kids scattered just out of view, waiting for their cue to begin.

Taking in the moon, Elizabeth marveled at the sudden possibility that her mother watched from somewhere beyond that opalescent disk. She pushed away from the thought and focused on the task at hand.

After smearing fake blood onto her face, courtesy of

one of the adequately dressed zombies, Elizabeth stepped into the floodlights of the construction site where the men worked hastily, resolute on Hallow Forest's destruction.

Elizabeth's blood-curdling scream took residence in the ears of every member of the construction crew. The machines rumbled and died. With equal parts curiosity and apprehension, a crowd formed in front of her. Scrum let loose a howl that managed to send a tremor down Elizabeth's spine.

"You have to help them," she pleaded to her new formed audience. "We got lost in the woods. It's haunted. Everyone knows you can't go into the woods, but it was a stupid dare. Please. Will you help?" Elizabeth's words strung together into one breathless sentence.

Some of the crew whispered Elizabeth's name. She caught words like, odd, and orphaned, and, liar.

Just then, a familiar voice reached her ears. "She's lying, Papa. She's that town freak who makes things up to cause trouble. She's the one I told you about. Telling everyone she's made friends with a witch in the woods!" "This is her?" The man with the salt and pepper beard pulled through to the front of the gathering, trailed by Susie. "She's the one I caught stealing the keys from the equipment. Is that, is that blood on your face?" His eyebrows pinched to the center of his face, his hand forming a fist over his mouth, while he tucked Susie closer, angling his body like a barrier in front of her.

Elizabeth's jaw clenched, and heat rose inside her, hot enough to make Franny's cauldron bubble. She needed to stick to the plan.

"They'll die if we don't hurry."

Her plea peeled their attention from Susie's father back to Elizabeth.

"Where?" Someone asked.

It was what Elizabeth waited for, the tug on the hook. Now she had to yank. "This way. Hurry."

She rushed back the way she came, back into Hallow Forest. She could hear varying degrees of concern from the men about going back into the woods, but they soon followed.

Elizabeth kept in their line of sight until she reached the predetermined checkpoint, where she promptly ventured behind a thick tree trunk and crouched out of view.

A few more steps, come on, Elizabeth mused to the work crew, especially to Susie who had refused to stay behind and now trailed her father.

When Elizabeth's followers were in place, a girl ran out from the shadows, holding a hand over her eye, pleading and sobbing for their help. A few workers rushed to aide Jordan, but they stepped back in horror when she revealed a dangling eyeball behind her cupped hand that dripped red goo. Jordan held her hands out like a zombie, moving toward the group of adults. Three steps forward and Jordan tripped on cue. "Help," she croaked. "Help, me."

A young man, lean and utterly horrified, reached for her. But she was dragged backward before his hand connected. Jordan clawed at the ground as an unseen force pulled her into the umbridge, her screams promptly quieted once out of sight.

"Where is she!" the young man yelled.

It was working. Now, time to get them moving.

A howl filled the air. The men lifted their hardhats to better see the night sky, where a mass of lightning bugs churned against the star-speckled sky. Even Susie stood transfixed. What they failed to see was the cache of black bugs twisting among the dead trees. Their directive: land on any exposed skin. And they hit their mark well. Arms swung in the air as the bugs bit into flesh and tangled into hair and beards. Flashlights and headlamps sent distress signals in all directions. No one stuck around long once the attack began. Susie was the first to take flight, and her father followed suit. The others fell in line with their boss.

The bugs had done their job, and now everyone was on high alert, shifting and searching through Hallow Forest for the protection of their machines and false lights.

Jordan appeared next to Elizabeth, her teeth and lips blood-stained, forming a wicked smile. Together they followed in the wake of chaos to watch the rest of their plan unfold.

A sound like clattering bones came from overhead. None of the workers stopped to look above until tree limbs reached down like clawed hands, bending low to scrape the tops of their hardhats and grasp at their clothes.

Squeals erupted as a mesh of bodies pushed through this new horror. As they escaped the atrocity, they were greeted by snarling creatures that lurked behind trees with gnashing jaws. Monsters with multiple eyes growled from the ground near their feet, and banshees shrieked just out of view.

Of course, there were no real monsters. Elizabeth and Jordan collected their performers as they followed the crew. Each child beamed as they fell into step with the others, this being their best performance yet. And all the while, the men ran, Susie fastest of all.

Sir Skeleton was by Elizabeth's side but hidden just out of sight. He lent a hand down to Elizabeth and she took it. Lifted above the ground, she was carried away from her friends and set near the construction site.

"Franny would be proud of you, little witch."

Elizabeth beamed, but her smile fell when she thought of Franny, and of sweet Ghost. Were they gone forever?

Elizabeth removed the star-shaped vial from her pocket. One way to find out.

She emerged from the woods.

The crew was now back at the site, frightened words rising from their huddled group. "We need to call the police!" someone hollered. "We need to destroy the woods!" called another.

They yelled and argued, but no one left. Not yet.

Elizabeth pulled the stopper from the vial, pouring the sap over the dead roots of the trees. She ran around the site, dripping the entire contents of the bottle.

Arguments ceased when the ground began to rumble.

Elizabeth placed the empty vial into her pocket and stumbled back over the shifting dirt to meet up with Jordan and the other children inside the tree line untouched by the machines.

Thick roots shot out of the ground like monstrous wriggling worms, probing the open space from where their stems once stood. The roots coiled and turned into one another, anchoring themselves before their relentless pursuit to reclaim their land. The world went dark when the floodlights, perched atop three long poles, toppled and shattered. Once Elizabeth's eyes adjusted to the pale cast of moonglow, she watched as the roots raced across the newly turned earth, serpentine and searching, finding the metal beasts that had wrought their destruction. Like creeping vines, they ensnared the wheels, then reached up to grip the bodies in tight coils before slowly receding, dragging their prey into the ground.

Elizabeth's mother had taken her to see The Nutcracker two years ago, and watching the construction workers pirouette between roots, arms extended in an attempt to balance themselves as they leaped over the shaking ground, made her chuckle as she thought of her mother doing her best after the ballet to mimic the ballerina's movements.

Through it all, the smell of sap carried against the wind, sweet and earthy and rich with the promise of healing.

Within minutes, Hallow Forest was restored to its former haunted glory.

The watch on Elizabeth's wrist read 12:00. Her smile was a wild thing that grew as her friends threw their masks into the air, whooping and bouncing on their heels. The magic was over, but a tingling warmth lingered inside Elizabeth. A single ember lit from beneath the ashes.

***

Elizabeth's friends headed home soon after, talk of adventure and magic on their lips. Only Jordan and Elizabeth remained. Jordan pulled her into a tight hug.

"Here." Elizabeth unlatched the watch and handed it to Jordan.

"No. Keep it. That way you can set the alarm for tomorrow night's slumber party at my house. Six o'clock? Just after dinner?"

Elizabeth bit her lip and nodded.

"You know, it all happened so fast. But that was magic, right?" Jordan asked. "Like, real magic?"

"Someone once told me, there are many forms of magic. Maybe, we saw some tonight." Jordan nodded and took Elizabeth's hand, giving it a squeeze. "Come on. Let's go home."

"You go. I need a moment to say goodbye."

Jordan set her lips in a firm line but ultimately nodded and left Elizabeth alone on the hill.

Sir Skeleton and Scrum had disappeared into the night with no goodbye, and Elizabeth worried that their fates mirrored Franny and Ghosts. If not, she wished to say farewell.

She waited, but with no sign of her mystical comrades, she started home. A snap of a twig stalled her. Excitement brewed in her heart at the thought of seeing them again.

"Scrum?" Out of the shadows stepped an overstuffed pink princess dress. "Susie?"

Mud was smeared across her cheeks and clung to her lashes, twigs stuck out from her mangled hairdo like a crown. Elizabeth imagined she looked like goblin royalty.

"It was you!" Susie yelled. "You tricked everyone, but not me. I knew it was you. None of it was real. Your tricks won't save you from the police when I tell them what you did!"

Under the light of the moon, a shadow flew over Elizabeth's head and landed in the rat's nest of Susie's hair. Scrum clamped his hands on both sides of Susie's temples and leaned over, slobbering down her face while snapping his fangs.

Susie ran in circles, screaming before taking off toward town. Scrum leaped off her head before she ran too far and landed on Elizabeth's shoulder. They watched together as Susie ran, tripped, then rolled down the rest of the hill and out of view.

"Scrum! You're alright."

Scrum purred and whipped his tail.

"Did we do it? Are they all safe?"

Scrum focused on the woods, and Elizabeth followed his gaze, finding all manner of skeletons, witches, and ghosts now emerging between the shadows of the trees. Franny and Ghost were there. Ghost waved his little nubs eagerly. Franny gave a salute, and Sir Skeleton, removing his top hat, bowed. Elizabeth wanted to run to them, but as quickly as they came, they dissolved into the night. She couldn't be sure, but Elizabeth thought she glimpsed a flow of red hair over a purple velveteen cape.

Elizabeth's heart clenched. "Will I ever see you again?" she asked Scrum.

Scrum leaned over her and placed his little hand on her heart, giving Elizabeth his lopsided smile. He jumped onto a nearby tree and scurried out of view, leaving her alone. But she no longer felt the same burden in being alone, not as she had before.

Elizabeth promised to herself that she would return next Halloween, to see them again. Until then, forgiveness, truth, and kindness would be Elizabeth's keys, and there were many doors to unlock.

10. SCRUBBED
By JULIE JONES

Maryann ignored the Space Agency's "suggestion" that she stay in her room and went to the hotel bar for a drink instead. After the rough day she had, she deserved one last Earthly pleasure. Alcohol was prohibited in the Colony.

As she navigated downstairs and entered the bar, she noted the whole hotel was quiet. It seemed most of the colonists had opted to stay in their rooms as suggested, which suited Maryann just fine. She was in no mood for company, her nerves stretched tight as a drum head. She sat at the bar, nursing a rum and Coke, thinking dark thoughts.

She was a perfect candidate for this first wave of permanent settlers on Mars: a respected Bioengineer, unmarried, with no children. No family to speak of at all, in fact. Once she would never have envisioned herself as a pioneer, but Earth no longer held any charm. This place was cruel and unforgiving, and Mars represented a complete reboot of her life. She was ready to go.

The detachment exercises and other tasks that the Mars Colonization Board required for all colonists were easy for

SCRUBBED

her. Things like giving up all but 100 kg worth of personal possessions, closing all personal business, having all EarthNet communications implants removed, and deleting all user accounts. Maryann cleared up all her business in a long morning.

"Thanks for all your help," she told the tech nurse at the clinic. Her gratitude did nothing to assuage the dismay on the nurse's face. The woman removed the half-dozen microchips necessary with a sour expression and left in a huff.

The disconnect from the constant bombardment of EarthNet was jarring at first, but she embraced it. She found it a treat to be alone with herself inside her own skull, without the ongoing news alerts, trending topics, and social media pressures. The nurse tech would never understand the freedom she felt.

Even now, sitting alone in a hotel bar, she welcomed the solitude of her own thoughts. It made her sad to think how dependent humanity had become on technology, with the constant need for input and stimulus. Solitude, she found, is a delight.

She sipped her drink, allowing the warmth of the alcohol to relax her worn nerves. The frustration of unexpected delay gnawed at her, making her feel scattered and anxious. She longed to be aboard the spaceship, gazing out a tiny porthole at the stars and a receding Earth.

This colonization trip was no half-hearted attempt. The colony ship *Hermes* was fifty years in planning and construction. The huge cylinder, a design necessary to spin the ship for simulated gravity, could never launch from the ground. Landing the behemoth is also impossible. Space construction was the only option. For half a century, amateur stargazers watched the *Hermes* take shape through the eyepieces of their telescopes.

After decades of work and speculation, the colonists and the ship were ready. At least, the colonists were. Today's events landed her back in this blasted hotel, instead of her quarters aboard ship. She swirled her drink, watching the melting ice make patterns like plasma bursts in the dark rum.

"Good evening," a short, bald man said, passing her seat at the bar. She recognized him from her floor in the hotel. She nodded in response, glad he did not stop to chat.

Maryann would be joined on the long journey by over three hundred other colonists, all screened with meticulous precision. Less than fifty people were permanent residents at the moment, mostly engineers, specialists, and equipment operators, plus a few scientists. Hers was the maiden voyage of what was intended to be a three-year cycle of colonization trips between overcrowded Earth and the redder pastures of Mars.

The Mars Colonization Board turned over the actual work of getting the colonists onto the *Hermes* to the National Space Agency. The Agency, responsible for the daily transit between Earth and the Moon, was supposed to be most qualified for the job.

The Agency crammed all the colonists into hotels for a week before launch. The idea was for all the colonists to accustom themselves to the same time schedules before boarding the *Hermes*. It may have worked on paper, but the real-life result was cranky, nervous colonists, crowded conditions, and overworked hotel staff. It was an anxious, yet boring week.

The bar-bot hummed over on silent wheels to check on her. Unlike a human bartender expecting tips, it did not care that she was slow to drain her glass. It glided away and she sat up straighter, stretching muscles sore from the long ordeal of the day.

SCRUBBED

Things started out wrong and did not improve. First thing, the hotel's comm system failed to wake her on time, leaving her scrambling to catch up.

"Dammit!" A last-minute check revealed she was over the 100kg weight allowance. Not by much, but enough to annoy the Agency. They did not have a sense of humor about such things.

The extra time dithering over her too-heavy bags caused her to miss breakfast, only managing lukewarm coffee and a slice of burnt toast. She did not mind much, knowing how her belly reacts to freefall. She gulped it down and hurried to catch up with the others.

Thinking back now, she remembered the short, bald man that just passed her barstool was also in her launch group this morning. He was grumpy, standing in front of the hotel with the colonists waiting for the bus to take them to the launch pad.

"Why are we standing around out here?" he said.

"I could have slept in another half hour," a woman agreed.

The crowd muttered like sleepy bees in the early morning sunlight. A week cooped up in the hotel had not done much for their mood. Maryann worried about the year and a half they would be cooped up in the *Hermes* together.

Behind her, soft strains of *The Green Hills Of Earth* struck up on the bar's piano. Maryann turned in her seat, surprised to hear live music played by a human. Most hotels and restaurants used bots; human musicians were rare. Though he was not technically perfect like a bot would be, she appreciated the emotion the player put into his performance, a feat no robot could duplicate.

She turned back to her drink, the piano's notes melding into her memories of the day. The woman next to her on the bus had hummed the same song on the ride to the launch pad. It seemed everyone around her was waxing nostalgic for Earth, and they had not even made it off the planet yet. She could not wait to be gone.

Despite being a hoverbus, the ride to the launch pad jounced her in a kidney-bruising fashion. That was only the first abuse her body would take. The process to board the orbital shuttle *Grasshopper* felt interminable, standing forever in unmoving lines, sweaty and thirsty.

Space Agency representatives were on hand to herd the colonists aboard. Her throat was dry, back aching, and her feet sore by the time she made it to the entry hatch.

"Keep moving! Find your seat and latch in! Keep moving! Find your seat and latch in!" The Agents directing traffic were stuck on repeat. One scanned her ID badge and pointed toward the nose of the ship. Another was blocking the aisle, trying to help a colonist buckle her safety belt.

The air inside the shuttle smelled of disinfectant, sweat, and a curious burnt metal smell that Maryann understood was the scent of space itself. That is what the old space hounds claim.

At last she was in her seat, a heavily padded thing with a five-point harness. She was on the aisle, with another woman to her left in the window seat. Maryann considered asking her to switch seats so she could watch the Earth fall away as they launched, but rejected the idea. It felt like too much work after the arduous process of boarding.

The shuttle, loaded and ready, sat on the launch pad waiting for clearance to blast off. Time stretched out like taffy, the minutes feeling thin and unreal.

She shifted on her metal barstool, reflecting how even the contoured, heavily padded crash seats of the shuttle became uncomfortable after a few hours. People began to

SCRUBBED

grumble at the delay almost as soon as the last harness clicked into place. Their mutters rose like the hum of industrial drones approaching.

"This is ridiculous!" a lady behind her screeched, three hours into the wait. "My feet are asleep!"

"Lady, I wish the rest of you was asleep, too!" the man next to her said.

"You're one to talk! You've been hogging the arm rest this entire time!"

Their argument was lost in the upwelling roar of the angry crowd. The Agents in the cabin with the colonists kept their cool, but were looking ruffled around the edges when the Captain's voice cut into the din.

"Ladies and gentlemen," he said, "I'm sorry to inform you that Luna Station has scrubbed today's launch. We will not rendezvous with the *Hermes*. Please follow the directions of the Agents to disembark."

His last statement was swallowed up by the angry shouts of the colonists.

"I have to peeeeee!" the lady next to her in the window seat yelled.

Smirking at the memory of the woman's distressed face, Maryann placed a stasis field around her drink, left her seat and crossed the bar to the restroom. If she thought boarding the shuttle was an ordeal, it was nothing compared to disembarking. By the time she got off the ship she was desperate for the nearest restroom, herself.

Returning to her seat at the bar she found her drink undisturbed. She removed the force field around it and took a hearty gulp, mind preoccupied with what could have caused the launch scrub. The bar-bot whirred by and refilled her glass.

"What do you think caused the scrub?" was the main question among the colonists on the ride back to the hotel.

"It had to be something big," one man said. Several people rolled their eyes at the obvious statement.

"You want big?" another man said. "I heard it was a rebellion on the Moon, started by a one-armed man!"

"Oh, stuff a sock in it, Jerry!" a woman said. "You didn't hear squat. You've been busy getting off the shuttle and back on this bus, just like the rest of us!"

Maryann listened to their theories all the way back to the hotel. She had her ideas regarding the scrub but kept them to herself. She stirred her fresh drink, thinking.

There was no way to know how long it would be until the Agency could reschedule the next shuttle launch. She doubted it would be as early as tomorrow. Docking up with a ship like the *Hermes* was nothing like the easy leaps between Earth and Luna. She suspected a problem with the colony ship itself. The *Grasshopper* could have gotten them into orbit.

She was ready. Mentally prepared to leave forever and never look back. And yet here she sat, at loose ends and unhappy about it. She expected to be settling into her tiny cabin on the *Hermes,* on her way to a new life. Not stuck in a dim hotel bar with an uncertain future.

What to do with herself?

She made and discarded half a dozen plans, from calling old friends to finding a book store. Everything felt meaningless now. The Board had mandated that colonists cut all Earthly ties. No book or conversation with a former friend could fill up the empty hours she faced. She was trapped between two lives, with no forward momentum and no way to go back.

In this moment, she felt lost.

"Oh my God, Maryann? Is that you?"

The voice was deep and golden, like honey flowing over bread. It went into Maryann's ears and traveled along her spine, shivering her soul with its power. It was Richard.

Five years not hearing that golden honey voice. Five years of not looking into the endless blue depths of his eyes. Five years that felt to Maryann like five seconds, and a thousand years at the same time. Five years of hating him, and loving him.

She thought this Earthly tie was long cut. The thrill his voice sent into her system suggested otherwise.

"Richard?" she squeaked, staring.

"I can't believe it's you!" he yelled. He yanked her off the barstool to envelop her in a giant hug. He still used the same cologne.

"Yeah, it's me," Maryann said into his lapel. Her shocked brain was unsure how to further respond.

"This is crazy!" He let her go enough to get a good look at her face. "How are you? How have you been? Are you in the City for work? Can I buy you a drink?"

His barrage of questions did nothing to clear Maryann's head. He let her go and pulled out a barstool next to hers. She sat back down, feeling shaky.

"Drink?" he asked again, and she held up her almost full glass.

"Oh," he said, grinning, then ordered a beer for himself from the bar-bot. "So what are you doing here? Are you in town for work or something?"

"Something like that, yeah," she said. "I thought you were in Australia."

Richard flinched as if she hit him.

"Yeah, well," he stammered. "That didn't exactly...work out. I was only there about ten months."

"Oh. What happened?"

He gave a derisive snort. "That 'great job' I had lined up was a total bust. They completely inflated their earnings and lied about the product line, then couldn't follow through with the hiring agreement I signed. I guess they thought I'd be stuck there and just stay with them, but they thought wrong."

Maryann felt a small pang of glee that his fabulous plans had blown up in his face. She stifled it as best she could. Feelings connected to Earthly concerns were discouraged.

"Gee that's too bad," she replied, and downed her drink in two swallows. "I hate to hear that you shattered my heart and left me behind for broken promises halfway around the world." She failed to keep the bitter note out of her voice.

Richard's shoulders slumped. "I deserve that," he said.

"You do," she agreed, and stood up. "I'm going to bed. I'm glad you're doing well. Goodbye, Richard."

"What?" he said, jumping up. "We just now reconnected and you're going to bed?"

"I'm not interested in reconnecting," she replied, turning to go. He grabbed her elbow.

"I think you *are* interested," he whispered, pulling her close. "I think your heart is racing, just like mine. I think you believe fate brought us together tonight, just like I do."

Maryann stared at him.

"That's the stupidest thing I've ever heard," she said, and pulled her elbow from his grip. He stood there, mouth open like a fish flopping on a dock, as she went out the door. She was terrified he would follow, but no footsteps pursued her as she hurried for the lift. She escaped.

An Agent stepped out of a side corridor and blocked her path, stopping her short.

"Good evening," he said. It sounded like 'Hey you.'

"Good evening."

"I have a few questions before you go to your room," the Agent said.

SCRUBBED

"Questions about what?"

"Who is the man you spoke to in the bar?"

She hesitated, but there was no point in sidestepping.

"His name is Richard. We were a couple once, many years ago. It was a chance encounter."

The Agent looked doubtful of this. His frown made his eyebrows look like angry caterpillars.

"You are aware, of course, that any personal or familial tie to Earth is discouraged," he lectured. "This contact is forbidden for Colonists."

Maryann choked off a bitter laugh. "You think I *wanted* to run into him? Ha. If I could have avoided it, believe me, I would."

He was not deterred. "Further contact with this man is actively discouraged."

"Well if it's so discouraged, why the hell is your Agency letting civilians in the hotel at all?" she asked. She felt smug at his surprised face.

"Ideally, the colonists would be mostly vacated by now. Some aspects of the hotel's revenue have been impacted by the Colonists' residency here, for example the bar's income. We agreed the hotel could resume some of their normal activities today, but that order was rescinded when the launch was scrubbed. I'm afraid I will have to report both this security oversight, and your interaction with the man in the bar."

Her heart sank. This could jeopardize her eligibility for Mars.

The Colonization Board was immovable in their stance that colonists, at least the first few, required total separation from Earth to succeed and flourish. It was believed that psychological ties, even the smallest ones, would manifest in things like extreme homesickness, depression, or remorse. Colonists had to be fully invested in the program, or it would fail. The Board would not be amused with her one-in-a-million chance encounter with Richard.

The Agent scanned her ID badge and recorded a few details, then allowed her to escape to the lift. Her room felt like a luxurious haven of privacy. It was a false sense of privacy, of course. The hotel monitored everything.

She sat on the bed and ran nervous hands through her curly hair. Seeing Richard threw a kink into her mental state, a complication she would not have thought possible. Her determination to go to Mars was stronger than carbon fiber, but her unpinned emotions made that determination feel thin and flimsy.

Was Richard's ridiculous assertion correct, that fate had brought them back together? A rare launch scrub and an even rarer lapse in public security, all leading up to a chance encounter with the one person that could potentially make her rethink her Mars plans? Maryann began to wonder if refusing to reconnect was a mistake. Sick with indecision, she went to bed.

Sleep was broken and disturbed that night. The terrible scene five years ago in the restaurant kept playing itself out in her dreams, over and over again. Each time she seemed to see it from a new perspective; even once dreaming she was the server-bot that came to the table to offer dessert and overheard everything.

Every detail of her dreams were perfect. The muted tones of candlelight that seemed to glow from everywhere; the soft background music; she could even taste the food. Then came the Dreaded Moment. Even asleep she could feel it coming. If only she had that advantage five years ago.

Richard opened his mouth, and instead of saying, "Will you marry me?" he said, "I'm moving to Australia."

The shock, even in her dreams, was so thick she almost choked on it.

SCRUBBED

"What do you mean, 'moving to Australia'?" dream Maryann asked.

"I have a terrific job opportunity and they need me right away. I'm leaving next week."

Stunned silence hung like heavy curtains around the table. Dream Richard began to look concerned, as if perhaps she did not understand. He was right.

"What do you mean, 'a terrific job'? What do you mean, you're 'leaving next week'?" Her stunned brain was stuck on variations of the same question.

"I was recruited by their EarthNet HR rep," Richard said. "They're kind of a startup, but if I get in on the ground floor it can be a big deal in a few years."

"What about me?"

His face went slack, a detail she noticed even in the dream. He would not answer.

"What about *us*, Richard?" she said, louder. He made a shushing motion at her, but she ignored it. All restaurants have sound dampening fields around the tables, but in her dream they were the only occupied table in the place. She could be as loud as she wanted.

"How childish can you be, Richard? Did you even think about *us*?"

"Of course, I did," he said, defensive. "But I was pressured to make a quick decision, and I did. It would be great if you would come with me..."

She snorted in disgust. "I'm supposed to uproot my whole life with a week's notice? I didn't even know you were looking for a new job!"

"I wasn't looking! They found me."

"So somebody dangles a shiny in front of your eyes and you grab at it, without even thinking about what you're dropping in the process? Is that what I'm hearing?"

"Maryann, I'm not dropping you. I love you. I just said

I want you to come with me."

"See, it kind of sounds like you don't." Dream anger felt just as righteous as real life. "Because this is not the sort of thing that people in love do. They don't just announce they're moving halfway around the world with zero notice."

His cheeks were red and his forehead white, a sure sign he was angry. He was not getting his way, and that did not sit well with him.

"What *do* they do, Maryann?"

"I don't know!" She scrambled for an answer. "They get married!"

"And there it is!" he said, finger shooting out at her like a harpoon. "There's what you're really mad about. You thought I was going to propose tonight, didn't you?"

Her silence said it all. She barely kept her eyes dry.

"Sorry to disappoint you," Richard said. His tone was sincere. "If you must know, I intended for us to go to Australia, make some money, maybe get married there."

"Maybe? *Maybe* get married there? Richard, I'm not going to Australia," she said. "I've always appreciated your free spirit, but lately you've been acting like a spoiled brat. And for you to do something this rash worries me. What if you go to Australia and meet someone? What then? It was so easy to pick up and move continents, so what stops you from picking up and moving out on me?"

"What stops me is that I love you."

"Yes," she said. "And you love adventure, and your dog, and whitewater rafting. All those things you can have in Australia. But not me."

"And I'm not proposing. Not tonight."

"Will you turn down the job and stay?"

Richard sighed. "Maryann, I already quit my job here and gave notice to my apartment block."

"So that's that. You told your job and your landlord

SCRUBBED

before you told me. I guess I was in the top three, maybe."

She gave him a small smile and stood, folding her napkin.

"Where are you going?" he said. She let out a humorless laugh that seemed to echo around the edges of her dream.

"I'm not going to Australia, and you're not proposing," she replied. "Doesn't that mean we're through?"

"No! I don't want to lose you."

"I don't either. But I need a partner that's home every day and won't suddenly decide to change hemispheres on me. I'm sorry."

She rounded the table to press a kiss on his forehead, trying to avoid his pleading eyes. He said nothing as she retreated into the dreamy darkness around the table.

This nightmare cycle repeated itself over and over, and Maryann twisted her sheets in torture. When the hotel room's communication panel buzzed in the gray hours of morning, she woke with a jerk, sweaty and unrested.

The buzzing was annoying and loud. She sat up, combing her hair with her fingers in a futile attempt to look awake. The holographic clock on the bedside table read 7:13 a.m.

"Answer comm," she ordered the room's computer, and the buzzing subsided. The screen flicked to life, and Maryann's grainy eyes beheld the same Agent with caterpillar eyebrows that questioned her the night before.

"Good morning," he said.

"How can I help you?"

"You will meet with the Assistant Deputy Director of the Mars Colonization Board at 0830," the Agent said. "Please be in Conference Room C on the lobby level of the hotel by 0825."

"I assume this is regarding my interaction with the

civilian last night?"

"You are correct," Caterpillar Brows said. "Do not be late."

"I'll be there," she said, and the screen went dark. She shuffled to the bathroom.

The shower felt like tiny needles poking at her skin. She welcomed the hot, stinging pain. This whole situation was ridiculous. The nightmares, while awful, had done a lot to help clarify her feelings. She still cared for Richard, but she had mourned their love long ago. Seeing him again did stir up her baser reactions, but her life's focus was now 150 million miles away, on a cold planet covered in rusty iron dust.

This morning she was going to battle to prove it.

She dressed and took care to make her hair look more under control, and less like she had gotten an electric shock. She put on her favorite lipstick and grinned at the mirror, surprised at how much her smiling face helped her feel more confident.

A quick jaunt through the breakfast line scored toast and coffee, and today she was early enough to get butter and jelly with it. On her way out of the dining hall she grabbed a water, drinking as she made her way to Conference Room C. A figure loomed next to the large double doors.

As she approached, she locked eyes with the same Agent for the third time. Maryann wondered if the man ever slept. He waited for her.

"Thank you for being prompt," he said. "Please hold your arms out to the sides."

She complied, and he poked his finger at the screen of his device. He scanned her for weapons and hidden technology. She was clean.

"You may enter. The Deputy Director will be with you

SCRUBBED

shortly. You will speak respectfully, but truthfully. Do you have any questions?"

"Not that I can think of at the moment."

He gestured to the door and she entered, discovering that Conference Room C was no larger than her hotel room and held only two long tables and half a dozen chairs. She took one facing the door, in the far-right corner.

Her wait was not long. The door opened to admit a man and woman, both well-dressed and poised. She was tall and elegant, with blond hair and chocolate colored eyes. The man was small and thin, with a weaselly face and a ring of scruffy hair clinging to the edges of his scalp. Each bore a badge with the Mars Colonization Board hologram. Maryann stood to meet them.

"Hello," the woman began. "I am Deputy Director Elizabeth Gordon. This is my colleague, Dr. Thomas Bergin."

"Hello," Maryann said. She noticed Dr. Bergin was carrying a small black box under one arm.

"Please sit," the Deputy Director said, and the three of them took chairs at the table, Maryann confronting the two officials alone.

"I'm going to begin by asking Dr. Bergin to explain what he has brought with him."

The Doctor placed the black box on the table. "This device is a Multispectral Autonomous Reaction Scanner, or ironically, M.A.R.S. It will scan you as we ask questions and measure your autonomous reactions, such as breathing, body temperature, brain reaction, et cetera. This happens across a range of spectrums, from infrared to x-ray. It also analyzes speech patterns and tone of voice, and body language."

"You want to know if I lie, is that it?"

"It's more than that," the Deputy Director said. "Your

automatic responses can give us valuable insight into your state of mind. Monitoring brain function is an important tool in understanding the workings of the psyche."

"Are you saying that box can read my mind?" she said. The woman laughed.

"No, not at all. But we can know with greater certainty whether or not you fully mean what you say. Sometimes the mind and the heart do not agree. Yours must, if you want to go to Mars."

"I already submitted to a battery of these tests during the screening process to become a colonist."

"Yes, and we will compare today's results with those," the Deputy Director said. "We are simply trying to determine that recent events will not affect your state of mind as a colonist."

"Okay," Maryann said. "When do we start?"

"I have been scanning you from the moment we entered," Dr. Bergin answered. This was not much of a surprise. She assumed it was some sort of recording or monitoring device as soon as she spotted it.

"Deputy Director," she began, and was cut off.

"Please, call me Ms. Gordon."

"Very well. Ms. Gordon, I want to make it clear up front that my interaction with the civilian last night was purely coincidental."

The woman's face was a mask of practiced neutrality. Maryann could read nothing in it.

"I read the report provided by the National Space Agency," Ms. Gordon replied. "The reporting Agent did his surface research and the data seems to support your statement. The Board asked me to look into it, and I checked your background for the last seven years."

"That seems like a lot of trouble."

"We have a vested interest in you, and this colony."

SCRUBBED

"Even so," Maryann pressed. "Forgive me, but this seems like a lot of hoopla."

Ms. Gordon exchanged a look with Dr. Bergin.

"Maryann," she said, "this endeavor, and its success, is more critical than you can know. It is vital we get this right, or the result is disaster. Let's be frank: once the ship leaves Earth's orbit, there is only the ship. The Colonization Board can't help you get along. The Board can't save you if something breaks. The Board can't magically bring you home if you decide pioneering isn't for you. So in effect, our job ends once you are on the *Hermes*. Until that time, we must ensure we have the best group possible to send to Mars."

She thought this over, but there was no sense in arguing. "I understand."

Ms. Gordon consulted her handheld screen. "You dated Richard Anderson for four years. Lived together three of those years. Owned one dog. Five years ago he quit his job, canceled his lease, took the dog, and moved to Australia. He remained there for ten months, three weeks, one day. You moved from Greater New York to New Atlanta four and a half years ago, where you worked for a private biotech firm, and lived until returning here for this launch. You changed all your user profiles, comm codes and online handles, and to our knowledge, never spoke to Richard Anderson again until last night. Would you say that's correct, Maryann?"

She felt a spike of astonishment. Dr. Bergin, absorbed in tending the small black box, made a huffing sound.

"Yes," she said. "And if you know all that, why am I being questioned?"

Ms. Gordon studied her.

"Are you aware that Richard Anderson has attempted to bypass the hotel security lockout and private comm your room four times since last night?"

Another huff from Dr. Bergin, noting her second blindside surprise.

"No," Maryann blurted. Her disbelief was plain. "I had no idea. He didn't get through."

"We know," Ms. Gordon said, only a little smug.

"I don't want to talk to him," she assured the Deputy Director.

"That's one of the things we're here to determine. Now, tell us about your history with Richard Anderson, please."

"Why is this relevant? We have not seen each other in five years."

Dr. Bergin cut in. "Frankly, we need to know what sort of person he is. Will he persist in attempting to contact you? Will he speak to the press? What effect will his interference have on your psyche?"

"Right now, the effect is that I'm annoyed with the launch delay and frustrated with this intrusion. Does your machine register that, Doctor?"

The ratlike little man blinked his beady eyes a few times and peered at the box.

"Actually, yes it does."

Ms. Gordon waved him to silence. "Please, tell us about Richard."

Maryann was helpless to protest. Her path to Mars now included this unfortunate interview.

"Richard and I met at a charity 5k," she began. The other two leaned in, Dr. Bergin to concentrate on his black box, Ms. Gordon to hear the details. "We ended up next to each other on the starting line. During the race he left me behind and I didn't think much of it. Then, at the end, I saw him just as I crossed the finish. He ran a 5k record time and waited around after, determined to find me again."

Dr. Bergin was quiet, watching his black box.

"He asked me to dinner that night, and I turned him down at first because he came off a little cocky. But he was sweet and persistent so I agreed. We had a lot in common, not least of which was a strong physical attraction. He was also orphaned by age fifteen, like me, and had spent a lot of time traveling."

Ms. Gordon nodded, encouraging her to continue.

"We spent a lot of time outdoors, camping, hiking, canoeing. He loves the wildlife preserves. After a year he asked me to move in. Everything was great at first. I caught on pretty quickly that Richard is impulsive and can be selfish, but these traits were more annoying than a real problem. Then I got promoted at work and my commute was long enough that I had to get my own place, nearer the university campus where I was doing my research. I would take the hyperloop to Richard's place on weekends."

"What was his reaction to this separation?" Ms. Gordon asked.

"He seemed fine with it," Maryann answered. "It was tough being apart at first, but we fell into a pattern that worked for a few years. My research grant was a three-year study, and it was winding down. I was expecting to give up my apartment and come 'home' within a few weeks when he dropped his bomb."

Dr. Bergin made a few adjustments to his black box.

"We had discussed my homecoming several times. It was our anniversary weekend, and Richard booked a table at my favorite restaurant. I thought he was going to propose, you see."

Ms. Gordon looked pained. She seemed familiar with this specific disappointment. "What happened?"

"He announced that he was moving to Australia,"

Maryann said. "He had already quit his job and notified his landlord. I had no 'home' to move back to, anymore."

"Why didn't you just go with him?" Ms. Gordon asked.

"It isn't that simple." She sighed. "Richard had been excessively reckless the last few months before we broke up. He was short-tempered and complained about almost everything. He was taking risks, rock climbing alone and without gear, disappearing for a few days here and there. He was always there when I went back on weekends, but he seemed restless and closed off."

"Why did that stop you?"

"Because as much as I love adventure, I love structure, too," she explained. "I like having a routine, and at least a rough idea what to expect. Large, unexpected shifts are hard for me to adapt to, and this shift was huge. I couldn't risk him taking me to Australia and doing something equally unpredictable."

"Perhaps Australia was what he needed," Ms. Gordon said.

"Perhaps it was," she agreed. "But it was not what I needed. And I could not deal with the fact that he would make such a life-altering decision without even mentioning it to me."

"It would be hard not to have lingering feelings, after something like that."

Maryann could see Ms. Gordon's strategy.

"Five years is a long time for lingering feelings," Maryann dismissed. "A part of me will always care for Richard, but I cut loose those ties long before I applied to go to Mars."

Ms. Gordon did not say anything, but looked to Dr. Bergin. He was still absorbed in the black box and whatever the tiny screen was showing him.

"Dr. Bergin," the Deputy Director prompted.

SCRUBBED

"Her feelings on the subject do seem firm," he said. "I can see no conclusive evidence that this interaction has done much more than inconvenience her."

"I told you," she said, unable to stop herself. "I want to go to Mars. Believe it."

Dr. Bergin punched a few commands into the black box, and then sat back in his chair. Ms. Gordon gave a slight nod and turned to Maryann. "These results seem to support the other data we have. Thank you for your time this morning."

"Am I to remain part of the mission, then?"

Ms. Gordon gave her a thin smile. "It is yet to be determined, but your chances are excellent."

This was the best she could hope for. "Thank you."

They parted ways, the two officials heading for the hotel exit like their heels were on fire, and Maryann wandered toward the lift. She pushed the call button and waited for it to come up from the basement level, mind lost in a replay of the meeting.

The lift doors opened to reveal Richard, wearing the same rumpled suit as the day before, his jaw shadowed with stubble.

"There you are!" he said, delighted.

"What are you doing here?"

He grinned like a fool. "Looking for you, of course!"

He held out a hand as if to help her step onto the lift, and looked confused when she moved back.

"You have to get out of here, Richard."

He stepped out of the lift, closing the gap between them. She stepped back again.

"But I just found you! I can't believe my luck. I gave the Brute Squad the slip and slept in my car so I could come look for you first thing this morning. I knew you went up to one of the rooms, but the hotel is booked solid and the stupid comm system wouldn't let me through."

"I know," she said. "What do you want?"

His look was incredulous. "What do I want? I want *you*. I want us! You never reached out to me after I went to Australia, and I looked for you in Greater New York after I came back, but you were gone. Now the universe has brought you back to me."

His eyes were dewey and soft, like a love-struck puppy. She felt repelled by the 35-year-old man-child that stood before her.

"Richard, we are over. I really need you to understand that."

He laughed. "No. No, we *were* over, but now we have a second chance!"

"No! We do not have a second chance!" she said, letting her exasperation leak into her voice. "We are not happening. Ever again. I'm sorry, Richard, but that's how it's going to be."

His face said this concept was out of his grasp.

"I've changed a lot in five years," he said. "I know we argued a lot the last few months we were together, and I realized you were right about a lot of stuff. I was really immature and totally self-centered. I was impulsive. I didn't value your feelings enough. I get that now, and I worked on those things. For you."

She felt like a rat in a trap. Richard's ears heard, but he did not listen. That much had not changed.

"I'm glad you worked on those things. But we are over."

Confusion painted his features. "But I love you."

"I know," she said, desperate. "And I know you can't understand why you're not getting your way. Look, you're going to get me in trouble. You have to leave now. And you can't come back!"

SCRUBBED

"Get you in trouble? How?"

For the first time, he took a good look at her. He took in her blue, standard issue Space Agency jumpsuit and the Mars Colony hologram on her ID badge. She heard the links connect in his mind.

His voice went dark. "What is going on here, Maryann?"

There was a long, ominous pause.

"You're one of the Mars Colonists, aren't you?" His tone was accusatory, as if she had been keeping a secret from him.

"So, what if I am, Richard?" She was angry with the situation. Why did the launch have to be scrubbed? This could all have been avoided.

"You're going to *Mars*? Geez, even I only went to Australia! You can't just leave forever!"

"I can't just leave forever, eh?" she scoffed. "You don't like the tables turned, do you? Well you see, I already quit my job and told my landlord."

"Damn Maryann, I'm sorry!" he shouted. "I made the biggest mistake of my life five years ago and now I've found you again, so you think I'm going to just let you go?"

"Yes, you are," she said. "Because my future isn't here anymore, Richard. And it isn't with you. I'm sorry. And you have to go now, before you ruin my life a second time."

The sound of running feet echoed up the corridor, Agents brought by Richard's shout. Maryann recognized the one she now thought of as "her" Agent, leading the pack as they rounded the corner of the hallway. His caterpillar eyebrows were angrier than ever.

"Sir, step away," he ordered. Richard stared at the knot of men in confusion.

"Why?" he asked. "I thought they couldn't talk to the press. I'm not the press."

"Step away, sir," the Agent repeated, and the group advanced.

Richard backed away, hands held out from his sides. He shot Maryann a pleading look, but she did nothing to intervene. She removed herself from the scene, backing off to stand in a nearby corner.

Her Agent busied himself reporting to someone unseen on the other end of a comm link while the others surrounded Richard, hands above his head. The Agents each conducted their own security sweep, ensuring he had no weapons, recording devices, or illicit items. Satisfied that he was clean, they began questioning.

She remained in her corner, watching. Richard begged the Agents to let him talk to her. They ignored his pleas. He gestured with frustration, desperate to explain his position.

Three men from the hotel security staff joined the melee with the intent of taking their target into custody. Richard was unhappy with the new arrivals, and left off trying to convince them of anything. He began yelling at her over their heads.

"Maryann! Tell them it's okay if I talk to you!"

She felt like her mind was wrapped in wool, thick and fuzzy. The security guards began dragging Richard away. He was not making their job easy.

"Maryann! I love you! I will find you again! Mars isn't nearly far enough away to escape our love! Maryannnnnn!"

Her Agent stepped directly into her line of vision, his motion so sharp it seemed to cut Richard out of reality. His suited form muted Richard's pleas to a buzz, pulling some of the numbing wool away.

"My colleagues will escort him off the hotel property, and make sure he does not return," the Agent said. He took her elbow and led her away from the scene, releasing her as soon as they turned the first corner. There was another bank of lifts down the hall. "I don't know how he managed to evade security and stay on the grounds overnight, but I will find out. Are you okay?"

She was combing her hair with her fingers, trying to look less frazzled than she was.

"Oh yeah, I'm totally fine," she said. "I may have a stalker, and I'm worried about my standing with the Colonization Board now more than ever. But otherwise, I'm just great."

A tiny smile cracked one corner of her Agent's mouth. "The hotel cameras will have all the recordings of your encounter. Unless you were making plans to run off with him, you don't need to worry. And maybe not even then."

Maryann stopped walking. "What do you mean?"

He stopped and turned back to look at her. "You really don't know?"

She shrugged, ignorant.

"Look, you made it this far in the colonization process, right?"

She nodded.

"So you fit the criteria," he explained. "For this first bunch of colonists to go, you fit it better than most because they want the best of the best to get started. They make a big deal about 'no ties to Earth' and 'don't talk to the press,' but a lot of the threats they make if you don't comply are empty. They have already invested a lot of time and resources in each of you. You're going."

"So why scare me to death with the interview and all that?" she said, unsure if she should be angry.

"Because they *do* need to know if you're committed to this or not," her Agent replied. "You're a valuable asset so you'll go, regardless. But if they think you're not in it all the way, you're going to be watched, and assessed. As far as I know, you passed their test this morning."

"How much of that will be changed by Richard's magic appearing act?"

"It won't help your case, but once they review the hotel footage, you should be cleared." He cocked an eyebrow. "Unless...you *were* planning to run off with him?"

"Of course not," she said. "What will happen to Richard?"

The Agent's features went flat. Maryann's father had called it a "poker face." She could read nothing, and it was disturbing.

"As I mentioned, he will be removed from the hotel grounds and steps will be taken to ensure he does not contact you again."

He escorted her back to her room, gave a curt farewell at the door and disappeared down the corridor. It was only 9:45 in the morning and Maryann felt wrung out. She entered her room, intending to lie down and nap the rest of the morning away.

On the hotel's comm panel, in large black letters, read the message:

LAUNCH MISSIONS RESUME TOMORROW MORNING, 0800 HOURS

She collapsed on the bed in relief and fell into a deep sleep.

***

Three years later, a loud knock sounded on Maryann's apartment door, deep in the East Tunnel of Marsopolis. She opened the door to reveal a Colonization Board courier, holding out a package. The *Hermes* arrived that morning, bearing the second wave of colonists and a limited number of specialty imports requested by the Mars

SCRUBBED

citizens.

Maryann had requested a book, *Podkayne Of Mars*. It was a favorite from childhood, and felt even more poignant now. The courier handed over the brown paper-wrapped package and left. Inside she found a lovely old paperback copy of the Heinlein classic, in excellent condition considering its age.

She flipped through the pages, enjoying the faint smell of an actual book. A small slip of paper fell out and fluttered to the floor. She picked it up and unfolded it.

Dear Maryann, it began.

How wild to use paper to send a message, right? So 21st century! It's like you're a real pioneer. I had to pay to smuggle this note to you. I've been working very hard and studying, and last week I submitted my application to come to Mars! I'm looking for the right people to pull some strings and get me through the screening process so we can be together again. I told you I would find you! Love always, Richard.

ABOUT THE AUTHORS

Paul G. Buckner is an Amazon Top 100 selling author, a Cherokee Nation citizen, musician, and an avid outdoorsman. He attended Northeastern State University and holds a bachelor's degree in Business Management and a Masters of Business Administration. He lives in Claremore with his wife Jody and son Chase.

Mark Cook, creator of Last Wednesday Writers, is a member of the Cherokee Nation and holds a bachelor's degree in journalism from Northeastern State University. Mark has taught English for fifteen years at an at-risk high school and has taught photography to adults for ten years. He is married to his wife Lisa and they enjoy their four dogs together in Pryor, Ok.

Aarika Copeland is the author of several short stories published through various online media. She has three children, whom she affectionately refers to as fire-breathing dragons. She is married to her high school sweetheart Jon, and enjoys reading and writing when she's not battling cute and ferocious dragons. She lives in Claremore.

Julie Jones is a contributor to many freelance blogs, which she has enjoyed for the last few years. She lives in Claremore with her husband of sixteen years, Steve, and their two children. She enjoys reading, writing, the outdoors, and painting.

John D Ketcher Jr is a Cherokee Nation citizen, a retired U.S. Marine Gunnery Sergeant and a retired UMC minister having earned a Masters in Divinity at St. Paul's School of Theology in Kansas City, Mo. He has been married to his wife, Paula Ruth, for the last thirty-eight years. Together they have four sons, eight grandchildren and one great grandchild. He enjoys reading and woodcarving, and lives in Pryor.

10511208R00131

Made in the USA
Lexington, KY
27 September 2018